ASPECTS
OF THE
SCREENPLAY

ASPECTS
OF THE
SCREENPLAY

Techniques of
Screenwriting

Mark Axelrod

HEINEMANN
PORTSMOUTH, NH

Heinemann
A division of Reed Elsevier Inc.
361 Hanover Street
Portsmouth, NH 03801–3912
www.heinemanndrama.com

Offices and agents throughout the world

The author and publisher wish to thank those who have generously given permission to reprint borrowed material:

Excerpts from *Anatomy of Criticism* by Northrop Frye are reprinted by permission of Princeton University Press. Copyright © 1957 by Princeton University Press.

Excerpts from *Hero with a Thousand Faces* by Joseph Campbell are reprinted by permission of Princeton University Press. Copyright © 1961 by Princeton University Press.

Library of Congress Cataloging-in-Publication Data
Axelrod, Mark.
Aspects of the screenplay : techniques of screenwriting / Mark Axelrod.
p. cm.
Includes bibliographical references.
ISBN 0-325-00204-5 (acid-free paper)
1. Motion picture authorship. 2. Dialogue in motion pictures. I. Title.
PN1996 .A97 2001
808.2'3—dc21
00-059670

Editor: Lisa Barnett
Production: Elizabeth Valway
Cover design: Darci Mehall, Aureo Design
Manufacturing: Louise Richardson

Printed in the United States of America on acid-free paper
05 04 03 02 01   DA   1 2 3 4 5

CONTENTS

AND NOW FOR SOMETHING COMPLETELY DIFFERENT . . . AN INTRODUCTION

THERE HAVE BEEN A LOT OF BOOKS WRITTEN ABOUT SCREEN-writing, so what makes this one any different? Clearly, most of the books will tell you basically the same thing. After all, the one thing that any screenwriter is working with is story line, and for the most part story line is what sells screenplays. Story line is what gets pitched. The concept gets pitched. The "what's it about?" gets pitched. No one enters a pitch session and starts to discuss dialogue, even though the dialogue may be excep-tional and even though without dialogue one cannot have a screenplay. And though books may tell you that the three-act play is dead and that there are really five acts or nine acts or twelve acts, the one thing that remains constant in every standard screenplay is that it has a beginning, a middle, and an end, usually in that order. Aristotle knew that better than most, so I will begin with Aristotle soon, but now I come back to the ques-tion initially posed: What makes this book different than the others?

To that question all I can really answer is that it is based on the fol-lowing propositions: story line may sell the script, but structure and dia-logue will carry it off. To that end, this book spends considerable time on both structure and dialogue, the latter of which is an aspect of screen-writing that generally gets ignored by most other how-to books. As a mat-ter of fact, after reviewing most of the best-selling books on screenplay writing, I have discovered that the number of pages devoted in any one book to the craft of dialogue writing is meager indeed, often none at all. It's odd that although the standard 120-page script is filled predomi-nantly with dialogue, the craft of dialogue receives such little attention.

Part of that lack of attention may be due to the fact that most writers of screenplay books don't write much dialogue or may not have an approach to analyzing dialogue that would be of value to a screenwriter. But the irony is that some of the best screenwriters are those who have a clear understanding of screen dialogue and the techniques used to achieve that dialogue. Alvin Sargent, Buck Henry, Tom Stoppard, Richard LaGravenese, Christopher Hampton, and the late Steve Tesich and Waldo Salt are and were keenly aware of how to write screen dialogue using the fewest words with the greatest impact.

This is not to say that dialogue is the only thing that will be treated here. Attention to form and structure, to different approaches to form and structure, will be dealt with as well. I'll deal with people that you may have heard about, like Joseph Campbell, and people you probably haven't, like Northrop Frye. And just as I'll begin with what every book on screenwriting should begin with, Aristotle's *Poetics*, I'll finish with what every book should end with, namely comments on the life of a screenwriter.

I have included exercises at the end of each of the chapters, but exercises do not replace the act of writing. At some particular point, possibly before you've read this book and certainly after, you will have to sit down and write a script. I'm reminded of something the French screenwriter Jean-Claude Carrière wrote: "The screenwriter works hemmed in by a throng of technical constraints and commercial demands. He commits himself to a project that must necessarily be transformed beyond all recognition. Denied the novelist's comfortable introspection, he is usually required to describe his characters from the outside in. He knows his work is doomed to disappear; he himself is usually unknown to audiences, even by name. He therefore spends much of his life asking, 'How can I ever give expression to who I am? How can I—like other, better-known artists—make my voice heard as well?' " (1994, 185). To that end, we're all screaming in silence. I'm hopeful that, perhaps, this book will enable you to be heard or at least hear yourself.

To take full advantage of the book it would be useful for you to be familiar with or to screen the following films: *Rocky*; *The Cook, the Thief, His Wife and Her Lover*; *Rain Man*; *Citizen Kane*; *The Big Chill*; *Ordinary People*; *Breaking Away*; *Four Weddings and a Funeral*; *Romancing the Stone*; *The Name of the Rose; The Fisher King; One Flew over the Cuckoo's Nest; The Graduate*; and *Pulp Fiction*. This is not to say the book won't be useful if you don't screen those films, but to get the most from any book on screenwriting, there has to be a balance between the written word and the visual medium on which the word is predicated. In other words, to read something is one thing, but to see how what the word suggests is practiced is quite another.

So, without further delay, I now introduce two of the better-known actors in Hollywood film: Aristotle and Sylvester Stallone.

Mark Axelrod
Orange, California

ASPECTS
OF THE
SCREENPLAY

1

SCENE

From Aristotle's Poetics to Stallone's Rocky

THE ACADEMY AWARD–WINNING SCREENWRITER WILLIAM Goldman (*Butch Cassidy & The Sundance Kid*, *All the President's Men*) has written, "The important thing about a screenplay is that screenplays are structure that's all they are" (Sanders and Mock 1981, 18). Goldman has also said that structure is "simply making the spine, and you must protect that spine . . . you must decide what that spine is and . . . keep it clean. You can ring in invention, you can ring in surprise, but you better damn well very clearly connect it to the spine so the audience knows where it is" (18–19). If we can believe Goldman—and there's no reason not to—structure clearly plays a major role in the craft of the screenwriter. But the question we have to ask ourselves is this: Is that structure simply something that has been created by Hollywood, or does it go beyond the film borders of California?

To that extent, this book will focus on how screenplays are structured, and not just Hollywood screenplays, but the great majority of feature screenplays. In economic terms, there's a kind of script monopoly at work that transcends any particular film culture. This approach to screenwriting is basically the same whether one is writing with directors in mind like Robert Redford (*Ordinary People*) or Peter Greenaway (*The Cook, the Thief, His Wife and Her Lover*) or with actors in mind like Arnold Schwarzenegger (*Twins*) or Kenneth Branagh (*The Gingerbread Man*). Since screenplay structure really transcends any one particular film culture, we should take a look at where it all began. The art of narrative storytelling has its roots in song, a method of telling tales that predates the act of writing. So, perhaps, the best screenwriters were really songwriters or at least song tellers, singers of tales and the best of them was, of course, Homer, whom Aristotle knew well. So because screenplay structure is fundamentally dramatic and because drama is really the source of screenwriting and because the best place to begin is in Greece, the best Greek to begin with is Aristotle.

We can first begin with Aristotle's notion of tragedy, which he defines as "a representation of an action that is worth serious attention, complete in itself and of some amplitude; in language enriched by a variety of artistic devices appropriate to the play; presented in the form of action, not narration; by means of pity and fear bringing about the purgation of such emotions" (trans. S. H. Butcher 1951, 240). Now let's take these items individually. For our purposes, we can say that something is tragic if it "engages one emotionally." Most studio accountants would agree with that notion of tragedy, and in the course of box office history, films of the human interest variety, which are fundamentally grounded in tragic drama (e.g., *The English Patient*, *Ordinary People*, *Terms of Endearment*, *Prince of Tides*, *Il Postino*, *As Good as It Gets*, even *Babe*), have made more money as a genre than any other category of film. Aristotle's idea that tragedy is a "representation of an action that is worth serious attention" is painfully relative because what is worth serious attention to one producer is not necessarily worth serious attention to another. Let's say that the type of screenplay you want to write is one that you think is serious or has serious potential. That would be a good point of departure.

As far as being "complete in itself and of some amplitude or fullness," Aristotle is thinking of unity of plot. Homer's *Odyssey*, he says, was constructed around a single action and so, too, must the plot of a screenplay be representative of a unified action. In other words, if the presence or absence of something makes no apparent difference to the plot, it's not a real part of the whole, and if it's not a real part of the whole, it's not needed. As we'll see, this is a rule Stallone follows almost to the letter. But what then is a *whole*? A whole is that play which has a clearly defined beginning, middle, and end, usually in that order. For Aristotle, well-constructed plots neither begin nor end in a haphazard way and neither should screenplays. In most standard feature films that rule is etched in stone and the most financially successful box office films have been those that have clearly defined openings, progressive middles, and conclusive endings. As a matter of fact, Aristotle writes that neither beginnings nor endings should be arbitrarily chosen, and he prescribes a strict sequence of cause and effect. That specific sense of cause and effect, of some kind of inward connection, not only tends to satisfy the need for a whole script but also the audience's desire for comfortability and completion. In other words, films based on the work of E. M. Forster (e.g., A *Room with a View, Maurice, Howards End*) or Henry James (e.g., *The Europeans, The Bostonians*), which have a strong adherence to well-defined story lines, are more easily adaptable to an audience's desire for completion than a film based on the rather eccentric postmodern work of Samuel Beckett. As a matter of fact, the number of postmodern texts that have been adapted to feature films is slim indeed and those that do get adapted are often adapted to the point that their "postmodernism disappears" (e.g., *Name of the Rose, Lolita, Clockwork Orange*). Likewise, most of them as well as others (e.g., Antonioni's *Blow-Up*, Bertolucci's *Spider's Strategem*, García Márquez's *Eréndira*) have little or no U.S. financing behind them. So, the films that generally tend to get taken seriously are usually those films with accessible story lines that are also structurally integrated with many of those Aristotelian components.

So this unity of plot, as Aristotle has called it, is maintained in two distinct ways, by:

- the creation of a causal connection that binds the parts together (i.e., the way scenes connect to other scenes and sequences to other sequences)

- the creation of a series of events that are directed toward a single end

In other words, the action of the entire script tends to converge on a single point. Or as Aristotle says, "The thread of purpose running through it is more marked. Minor effects are subordinated to the sense of an ever-growing unity. The end is linked to the beginning with inevitable certainty and in the end we discern the meaning of the whole" (276). This statement is fundamental to screenwriting structure, especially the idea that the end is linked to the beginning with inevitable certainty. In effect, it's what Goldman means when he talks about the spine of the story. The one rule any screenwriter needs to keep in mind is this connection between how a film begins and how it ends and the dramatic interrelationship between the two (see *Scene Two*).

Aristotle continues to write that the play is written "in language enriched by a variety of artistic devices appropriate to the play; presented in the form of action, not narration." Certainly here we can take the liberty of asking ourselves, what are artistic devices appropriate to the play? That answer would, of course, depend on the content and context of the play, and it is here that Aristotle finally gives the screenwriter a bit more creative latitude with what he or she wants to write; however, the creative devices one employs in a script may or may not remain after the final cut.

Aristotle continues to say that a play imitates action and that action is brought about by actors who display both character and thought. As we've seen, he defines the representation of action as *plot*, or the ordered arrangement of incidents, and that ordered arrangement contributes to the unity of the plot, but he defines *character* as that bit of individuality that allows us to define the nature of the actors. Further, *thought* is the ability of the actors to say what is possible. Though Aristotle says the change in fortune must be from prosperity to misery, he's specifically dealing with Greek tragedy and not commercial tragedy. The former is exclusively Greek, the latter predominantly, but not solely, Hollywood.

According to Aristotle, then, plot is the most important item in dramatic presentation and in the representation of action, and within the plot he addresses two major points:

- reversals (a change of affairs from one situation to another)
- recognitions (a change from ignorance to knowledge)

These two items tend to broaden the scope of the plot and expand the action. Aristotle differentiates between simple plots and complex plots. Simple plots have no reversal or discovery, while complex ones do. To that extent, all standard feature screenplays are complex, even though the story line may be extremely simple, since a change of affairs from one situation to another over the course of the film is axiomatic (see *Scene Two*). But these reversals should develop out of the very structure of the plot so that they are the inevitable or probable consequence of what has preceded them. And though Aristotle had in mind that the reversal works *against* the hero rather than *for* him, the notion of reversals has become a mainstay of the screenwriter's craft.

Recognitions are situations in which the protagonist comes to terms with the truth, at least, the fictional truth. In *Rocky*, the recognition finally comes during the championship fight when Rocky realizes the truth that he no longer needs to worship Apollo Creed but can actually fight him. Regardless of what Woody tells Buzz Lightyear in *Toy Story*, the latter refuses to believe he's a toy. It's only when he realizes he can't fly that he accepts the truth. In *As Good as It Gets*, Melvin Udall, Jack Nicholson's character, realizes the truth that he cannot live without Helen Hunt's character, Carol Connelly. Pick a film, and you'll find a recognition. So, reversal and recognition become instrumental tools a screenwriter uses to fashion the structure of a script.

Finally, Aristotle writes that all of the items I've mentioned somehow are resolved "by means of pity and fear bringing about the purgation of such emotions." In other words, one may feel a certain amount of compassion for the character and have a certain amount of fear for the character, but by the conclusion of the script we, as readers, have somehow purged ourselves of such emotions by witnessing them occurring in our hero. That may or may not be what happens to you after you've finished reading a script or come out of a movie theater, but at least for Aristotle, something in the process of witnessing the act should have a kind of cleansing effect on the reader or viewer.

Concluding Aristotle's scheme, after thought comes *diction*, the expressive use of words; then *music* and, finally, *spectacle*. So as we've seen, not only has Aristotle defined screen tragedy for us, but he has also emphasized six items that are prominent in any screenplay:

- plot
- character
- thought and diction, which we can consolidate into dialogue
- music, which we can call the score
- spectacle, which we can call special effects

A word of caution here: In most instances, Aristotle was talking about popular feature filmmaking; anyone who has seen the work of Tarkovsky or Godard, Buñuel or Resnais would realize that Aristotelian rules don't apply in exactly the same way as they do with Stallone. The apparent anomalies don't entirely negate Aristotle's rules; they only modify them. That's a critical point to understand because whether the storyline is owned by Disney or is directed by Peter Greenaway, each is constrained by one common cinematic problem: screen time.

In terms of time, Aristotle knew that about two hours was the longest one could sit before a retsina break and what Aristotle and Hollywood have in common in this regard is the actual duration of the screen/play. Curiously, the standard feature film today is about two hours long. As a matter of fact, the average feature film hasn't changed much in terms of running time in forty years! These are not hard statistics, but if we use the first sound film, *The Jazz Singer* (1927), as a point of departure we can see that between 1927 and 1942, American films ranged from about forty-two to seventy-five minutes (though there were some films running between seventy-five and one hundred, at that time), with the average feature running at about sixty to seventy minutes. By about 1948, more and more films were running between seventy-five and one hundred minutes, and by 1953, the sixty-minute film had all but disappeared, yielding to the ninety-minute film. At the same time, the number of 100- to 120-minute films was also beginning to increase, and by the early 1960s, one sees a clear pattern of films running between 100 and 120 minutes, a length that has remained fairly constant through today, four decades later.

The reason for this particular length, of course, is not due to a refreshment break, but to finances. The shorter the film, the more it can be exhibited; the more it can be exhibited, the more money it can make. So, the usual script runs between 90 minutes on the low end and 140 minutes on the high end. A film fewer than ninety minutes long today might annoy an audience that has to pay a rather exorbitant price for what it considers too little (there are exceptions to this: *Trainspotting* and *Ma Vie en Rose* are only eighty-nine minutes), but the days of the sixty- to seventy-five-minute feature film, as well as the double feature, are gone with the wind.

On the other hand, a film of more than 140 minutes might cut into the profit margin unless, of course, it happens to star Mel Gibson (*Braveheart*) or Kevin Costner (*Dances with Wolves*), in which case the actors allegedly used some of their own money to leverage the deal, or unless the subject matter seems so "titanic" that it takes more than two hours to deal with (*Titanic*). The result of all this commodification is that unless a screenwriter is also the director and/or producer, she or he is not totally free to write whatever she or he wants, but, in a way, is restricted by a kind of corporate earnings mentality. That's not to say a writer can't write a well-written, thought-provoking, dramatic script. That's been proven many times over, but regardless of what some may say about being creative, formulas tend to exist and they often exist to appease what producers feel will effectively work for an audience.

Speaking of audiences, Aristotle observed that owing to the weakness of the audience, a play with a happy ending generally passes as the best kind of play and is usually, but not always, a comedy. Unfortunately, what Aristotle had to say about comedy has been lost, but in many standard feature films, the happy ending can be part of a hybrid that has been called a "dramedy"—a somewhat dramatic plot with some comedic overtones or vice versa—which brings us back again to *Rocky*.

There are a number of items in the original *Rocky's* character that would have pleased Aristotle, since Aristotle wrote that characters should be good and their portrayal should be appropriate, lifelike, and consistent. Those are extremely important items to note because, as we'll see, they are often the cornerstones of character development in feature screenwriting.

ROCKY

In the first seven scenes (which take approximately eleven minutes) of the film version of *Rocky*, there are some significant items that all follow a kind of Aristotelian pattern that would coincide with what Goldman has referred to as the spine of the screenplay. Here I look at each one of these scenes from the film individually to see what, in fact, Stallone was attempting to do, then I look at the final script version to see what changes took place from script to screen.

Scene 1

In the opening shot of the film, we hear the rather majestic music that was written by Bill Conti, a film composer who worked sporadically before he scored the film and who now is never out of work. The music is the first thing we hear in combination with the boldly inspiring title, ROCKY, and the two of them in tandem elicit a kind of triumphal quality.

A superimposition establishes the time, November 25, 1975, and the place, Philadelphia. But it is the opening shot that is of critical importance, because it doesn't reveal a portrait of Rocky or anything associated with boxing, but instead a representational headshot of Jesus. As the camera pulls back, on one side of Jesus there is an alpha (symbolic of the beginning) and on the other, an omega (symbolic of the ending), while beneath the representation of Jesus we see the words *Resurrection Athletic Club*. The combination of the name of the club, the picture of Jesus, the alpha, and the omega is important because they actually set up the frame for the picture. The theme of the film is established in the opening shot because the film is clearly one about resurrection—Rocky's resurrection from a "bum" (a refrain we hear throughout the film) to a "champion contender" in a period of five weeks between Thanksgiving and New Year's, during the bicentennial year of the United States. In that sense, the story line also becomes Stallone's political statement about the United States and how anyone can make something of himself in a land of liberty and freedom.

As the camera gives us a view of the entire club, we see that it's smoke-filled, grungy, and poorly lit. Not only does that situate Rocky in a particular environment, but it also establishes the potentiality of change. In other words, the movement from one kind of environment (e.g., a seedy boxing club) to some place much more regal (e.g., the Philadelphia Spectrum) is set up at the outset of the film.

From the beginning we see that Rocky is fighting in a rather lackadaisical manner. Clearly, he is out of shape, out of breath, and, seemingly, out of talent. At the bell, Rocky drags himself to his corner. It's here that the dialogue first begins to shape Rocky's character. As Rocky's cornerman attends to him, he says, "You're fightin' like a bum. Want some advice?" to which Rocky responds by saying, "Water." The cornerman asks him again if he wants some advice, but the second time Rocky merely says, "Mouthpiece." So in a very succinct way, we have discovered something quite revealing about Rocky's character as well as about a theme of the film. First, it shows that Rocky tends not to listen to people, even though what they say may be in his best interest, and second, it begins the thread of the "bum" theme.

At the bell, Rocky drags himself out again, but during the second round, Spider Rico, his opponent, gives him a head-butt, causing his left eye to bleed. The action does three things:

1. The action initiates a kind of revival in Rocky, who, upon seeing the blood on his glove, suddenly goes into a rage and attacks Rico viciously, driving him to the canvas and beating him so badly the fight has to be stopped.
2. The attack indicates that Rocky prefers to use his left hand.
3. It preconditions the audience about Rocky's tendency to bleed.

All of these items—(1) that Rocky has the capacity for rage; (2) that, as a "southpaw," he fights in a rather unorthodox style; and (3) that he bleeds easily from the face—contribute to Rocky's character and precondition an audience for what may, and does, happen later on.

After the fight, Rocky climbs out of the ring and bums a cigarette from a crony, and as he heads toward the locker room, a woman yells out, "Rocky, you're a bum," twice. So the word *bum* has been used three times during the first scene and therefore becomes a key element in the overall scheme of the film. Inherent in the notion of being labeled a bum is conflict, and Rocky must deal with the conflict between what others think of him and what he thinks of himself. The bum theme, which actually inaugurates the film in the first scene, essentially closes the film in the next-to-last scene the night before the fight, when Rocky, after visiting the Spectrum, returns to his apartment and says to Adrian, "I just want to go the distance. If I'm standing, I'll know for the first time in my life I wasn't just another bum in the neighborhood." Rocky's statement effectively closes the bum theme and the result of the fight conclusively ends both his speculation and his inner conflict.

As we know, the word *conflict* not only means the "act of striking together," but also "the opposition of persons or forces that give rise to dramatic action." So we see that conflict is the main emotional tension in any dramatic event and the notion of conflict in a boxing film only accents this. The conflicts that take place for Rocky are both inner and outer, both psychological and physical, which allows for a wide range of dramatic possibilities. The entire scene takes approximately three and a half minutes.

Scene 2

The setting is the cheap locker room after the fight. Rocky walks in smoking a cigarette, goes to his locker and pulls out a well-worn, beige terry cloth robe with the nickname The Italian Stallion haphazardly sewn on the back. Then he sits down on the bench and starts to untie his shoe as he awaits the entrance of the promoter.

Spider, lying in the corner and drinking what appears to be a beer, says to Rocky that he "got lucky tonight," a comment Rocky refuses to dignify with an answer. This act continues to comment on his rather stoic, if not rather arrogant, attitude toward what others may say about him. After the promoter has paid Rocky and Spider, Rocky asks, "When do I fight again?" to which the promoter responds, "Maybe in two weeks. Call me," an answer that establishes the fact that if Rocky is a regular fighter there, he's not high on the promoter's list.

But the scene is significant for two main reasons. It establishes the following:

1. the state of the locker room
2. the condition of Rocky's robe

In terms of reflecting change in a character, there has to be a point of departure and a point of destination. In other words, there must be a contrast set up between where Rocky is now and where he will be going later. The locker room is significant in that scheme because, in the course of Rocky's change, he will go from dressing in the dilapidated changing room of the Resurrection Athletic Club to dressing in the ultramodern facilities of the Philadelphia Spectrum. Likewise, the tattered terry cloth robe will be altered into an elaborate, red-and-gold silk robe with the phrase "The Italian Stallion" elegantly woven in Italianate letters on the back. These changes will coincide with the changes that Rocky will inevitably go through during the course of the film.

This scene takes approximately one minute, for a total running time four and a half minutes so far.

Scene 3

The setting is a trash-lined street, probably in South Philadelphia and clearly in a working-class neighborhood. Rocky, walking alone in the chill of the November night, stops by a pet store and playfully taps on the glass as if to engage the puppies in the window. Recalling Aristotle's admonition about characters being good and likable, this action makes Rocky—at least in the United States—a likable character because anyone who likes or befriends animals, who can relate to animals, is a likable character.

This scene, which is seemingly insignificant, but which continues to expand Rocky's character, also takes one minute, putting the total running time at five and a half minutes.

Scene 4

The setting is another street scene, a corner in Rocky's neighborhood, where a group of Rocky's friends stand around an open fire on the cold autumn night and sing. It's apparent that Rocky knows who they are as he stops for a moment and shares a swig of wine with them. But what's of greater importance is what he says to them as he walks away. Addressing their singing abilities, he says, "You guys are getting better every year." It's an important statement because it continues to round out his character; the statement is an encouraging one and it shows that Rocky has concern, if not compassion, for others. The combination of having the capacity both to encourage others and show concern for others further shapes him as a likable character.

The scene is also one minute, making the total running time six and a half minutes.

Scene 5

The setting is inside Rocky's apartment, which, to say the least, is a bit seedy. He walks in, opens the refrigerator, closes it, takes a half-empty bottle of something (perhaps beer) off the top of the refrigerator, chugs the remainder, and tosses the empty bottle on the kitchen table. He then turns on a record player, which plays a scratchy kind of melancholy jazz, and immediately feeds his two turtles, which we discover are named Cuff and Link, and a goldfish named Moby Dick. He says to them that if they could sing or dance he wouldn't have to be doing what he's doing, which presumes that he doesn't like what he's doing when, in fact, he does. But the apparent concern for these creatures continues to reinforce his like-ability, which was established in Scene 3.

A poster of Rocky Marciano hangs over the mantelpiece to let us know that Rocky also has heroes, and one can see a few trophies on the mantelpiece as well. One can overlook the fact that Marciano is an Italian name and Balboa, Rocky's last name, is Spanish, presumably after the conqueror Vasco de Balboa. What remains important in Rocky's mythology is that he valorizes boxing's greatest undefeated, white heavyweight champion.

He then walks to a mirror, in which we see various photographs of his father and mother as well as pictures of a young Rocky in football gear stuck into the corners. At this point he practices some seemingly superfluous words about turtle food that we discover will pay off in the following scene. He fumbles with the words, not getting them right, then abandons the effort. He stares at one of the photos of him as a child, removes it, and looks at himself in the mirror. What's significant here is that Rocky is reflecting on something. It could be that he thinks about who he is now versus who he could have been, and implicit in that reflection is conflict.

Finally, Rocky returns to the refrigerator, retrieves a couple of ice cubes, goes to his bed, and attends to his wounded eye. The bed is significant because it's a single bed, which accents Rocky's loner character. Next to his bed, attached to the wall, is a crucifix, which implies that Rocky is religious, if not in practice, then in theory.

So the scene establishes a number of items important to Rocky's character: Rocky lives alone; cares for animals; has idols; remembers family; is reflective; and is religious. Much of that information has been communicated nonverbally. The scene reinforces Rocky's aloneness, a factor that is also reinforced in a number of subsequent scenes. Finally, it sets up a contrast between who he is now and who he will be after Adrian moves in, since she gives the apartment a "woman's touch."

The scene, the second longest so far, is two and a half minutes, which puts the total running time at nine minutes.

Scene 6

It's the next morning and the setting is the pet shop we saw in Scene 3. Rocky taps on the window again, then walks in. We now meet Adrian, Rocky's apparent love interest, who works in the store. Homely, cosmeticless, and bespectacled, Adrian is very shy. Rocky's first words on entering

are, "How are you? Full of life." She demurs. Rocky then begins the monologue he was practicing in the previous scene, which is a joke about the
turtle food: when the turtle food gets caught in the turtle's throat, Rocky
has to slap its shell and it gets shell-shocked. Adrian smiles but is too
reserved to laugh aloud. This situation is significant in that we have the
conflict of Rocky trying to be intimate with Adrian, but on Rocky's terms.
One must remember that Rocky has to be consistent in character and portrayal and his attempts at courting Adrian have to be consistent with that
kind of character.

At that point, the shop manager, who overhears the joke, makes some
comment about starting with the bad jokes early, while Rocky's attention
is taken by Butkus, a large, caged boxer. While he is playing with Butkus,
the shop manager orders Adrian to go downstairs and clean the cat cages,
which are a mess. Rocky watches Adrian leave, but his look is one of
annoyance and presumes that Adrian is too good for that kind of work.

That kind of disdain leads into the next line, as the shop manager says
that "Rockhead" has to pay for the food, and as Rocky walks out of the
door without paying, he says, "Crime don't pay," which segues into the
following scene.

This scene is also one minute, making the total running time ten
minutes.

Scene 7

The previous scene ends with Rocky saying, "Crime don't pay," which
segues into a scene in which—unless he's being ironic—Rocky has to live
up to what he believes in. The setting is at the dockyard, where we discover that Rocky earns his money as a "strong-arm" for the waterfront
loan shark, Tony Gazzo. After exchanging some dialogue with a few other
marginal figures, he starts to run after a particular dockworker. Once he
catches him, he throws him up against a fence before asking for the
money he owes Rocky's boss. The dockworker, Bob, pays him what he has,
$130, but he's still "seventy dollars light." Bob says he's broke but offers
his coat as partial payment. Rocky tells Bob that he's not emotionally
involved, and if Bob doesn't pay he's supposed to break his thumb. But
the fact is, Rocky *is* emotionally involved, and instead of breaking the
dockworker's thumb, which is what he's paid to do, he takes the money

he's got, returns the jacket to Bob, and says three times in parting, "You shoulda' planned ahead," as if to let Bob know that Rocky's done him a favor by not disabling him. In a subsequent scene, Gazzo is a bit put out by what Rocky didn't do and chastises him for not doing it, but the scene continues to shape Rocky's character as a compassionate person, one who's been down on his luck most of his life and who understands what that's like.

This scene, like most of the scenes before it, is one minute, making the total running time eleven minutes.

So in the course of eleven minutes, or almost 10 percent of the film, we have discovered a lot of things about Rocky and about the direction of the story. In terms of plot, we know that the film will deal with some aspect of boxing, an action that is conflictive, and that it will probably involve a character and situational change from bad to better that can also be conflictive. In terms of character, we know a number of things about Rocky: he's good, lifelike in dialogue and action, and Stallone's portrayal is, so far, believable and consistent. In terms of thought, we know, even in a nonverbal way, what kind of things Rocky thinks about, that is, what things are important to him: family, religion, friendship, love. In terms of diction, we know how the character speaks and what his language may reflect sociologically because his accent situates him in a particular socioeconomic milieu.

Now all of these scenes from the film have been so constructed as to give the audience a specific sense of Rocky's character. But is that what Stallone actually wrote? From the revised master scene script dated December 30, 1975, and January 5, 1976, to when the film opened in New York and Los Angeles in November 1976, one can see some startling differences between the scenes in the script version and the final cut, almost all of which have been dramatically revised to improve the film. As it is, the 1975 script is not very well written, and the fact that Stallone purportedly wrote it in five days may account for that.

For example, in the original script there are scenes that should have been expanded and weren't; there are scenes that didn't need to be there at all and are; and there are scenes that are out of order in terms of the functional linearity of the story. In addition, there are numerous scenes in which the dialogue is entirely overwritten and wasteful. So let's take a look at the revised draft of the script and study the same 10 percent of the script that we did with the film.

Scene 1

The opening scene has no allusions to Jesus, or alpha, or omega and takes place not at the Resurrection Athletic Club, but at the Blue Door Fight Club. Rocky is fighting a black boxer, not a Latino. As Rocky's black opponent dances and hits Rocky's face with great accuracy, "the punches do not even cause Rocky to blink . . . He grins at his opponent and keeps grinding ahead" (*Rocky* 1976, 1). This description of Rocky is in direct contrast to what we see in the film. In the film we see a thoroughly out-of-shape Rocky who is struggling just to stay on his feet while attempting to avoid the garbage that's being tossed in the ring by the fans.

Rocky's dialogue with the cornerman is fundamentally the same, though it's longer and wastes words. Rather than say, "Water," and "Mouthpiece," Stallone has Rocky say, "Just gimme the water," and "I just want the mouthpiece," both of which add nothing to the dialogue. The head-butt and Rocky's subsequent rage are included, but Rocky wears The Italian Stallion bathrobe in this scene, not in the next, and the scene finally ends with Rocky climbing out of the ring, bumming a cigarette, then fading "into the darkness of the rear of the club" (2).

So there are some significant differences between the final script version and the final cut. In terms of story line, there is no allusion either to Jesus or to the resurrection motif and though the cornerman says "bum" there is no repetition of the word from the woman outside the ring that would accent the bum theme. In terms of character, the script reflects a rather self-confident and intimidating Rocky rather than one who is clearly in poor condition in the film. The reason for the changes evident in the film will become more apparent when we discuss the arc in the next chapter, but suffice it to say that once again there needs to be a point of departure and a point of destination. If Rocky is in decent shape at the beginning, then there can be no contrast between who he is now and who he will become. If, however, Rocky is in poor shape in the beginning, there is the basis for contrast between where he begins and where he ends; hence, the revision in the film.

Scene 1A

The locker room scene is totally different. Rocky is already dressed and, along with three other fighters, awaits the entrance of the promoter. The promoter soon enters and pays Rocky, and Rocky leaves. Rocky says nothing in the scene. Moreover, nothing of which the promoter and the fighters say is of any importance to the story line or to Rocky's character. The dialogue has one fighter saying he's going to Atlantic City, and another fighter saying it's cold there, and the first fighter says because it's cold he'll have the city to himself. So one really needs to ask what this exchange has to do with anything. It does nothing to shape Rocky's character nor does it do anything to advance the story line, it merely exists to fill up time until Rocky is paid. However, the changes that were made in the final cut have altered the scene significantly and made it more important in terms of who Rocky is and where he is going. In other words, the dialogue as it reads has contributed neither to the overall structure of the script nor to the overall structure of Rocky's character.

Scene 2

This scene takes place on an almost empty trolley traveling to South Philly. Rocky is sitting near a "black woman," who, after studying Rocky's bruised face, causes a self-conscious Rocky to comment, "I'm a fighter," to which she replies, "Yo 'iz an accident" (3–5A). This scene is also wasteful. First, the scene description is illogical, because the fact that he's heading to South Philly would be information known only by a reader, not by a viewer, unless something in the scene were visually to indicate where Rocky is traveling. Second, in Scene 1, Stallone writes that Rocky is "unfazed" by the punches that land, and though he gets butted, it only affects the corner of Rocky's eye. Why, then, is his face so bruised in Scene 2 that a stranger would call him "an accident"? Third, the scene does nothing in terms of either advancing the story line or shaping Rocky's character. The fact that Stallone included it is curious because it seems to lack intention.

Scene 3

This "scene" has Rocky walking down the street and waving to some prostitutes. Rocky walks by an alcoholic who's sleeping in front of a "dirty bookstore," then carries the man into a "protective passageway" (3–5A).

Then he pauses at the "ANIMAL TOWN PET SHOP," where he "peers into the dark store and sees a sad, huge dog sitting in the window" (3–5A).

This scene has been modified in several ways, by:

1. eliminating the prostitutes
2. relocating the unconscious alcoholic from in front of a "dirty book-store" (presumably he means a pornography store) to a later scene
3. revising the pet shop portion

What's most significant here is that the part of the script that deals with Rocky's relationship to the prostitutes has been deleted. The reason that it's been deleted seems to be related to the fact that Rocky's knowledge of and participation with prostitutes would somehow undermine the character of the Rocky in the film. One can assume Rocky is not a virgin and one can also assume Rocky may even know prostitutes, but to see Rocky fraternizing with prostitutes might somehow stain his image and that might tend to distance him from an audience.

Scene 4

This scene takes place outside Rocky's apartment, which is located in a rather sordid section of the city. There are no street singers.

Scene 5

This scene takes place in the hallway of Rocky's apartment. According to the script, "The narrow hallway is painted olive brown. A single light bulb illuminates the gloomy corridor" (5B).

Both Scenes 4 and 5 seem irrelevant. Presumably they are here to establish venue. In other words, we need to know something about the neighborhood in which Rocky lives. However, that's already been established in Scene 3, so the following two scenes repeat the obvious. There's no need for Scene 5 at all because we're going to see Rocky in his apartment in Scene 6, a scene that's more important in terms of shaping his character and reflecting his environment than the color of the paint on the hallway walls.

Scene 6

Now Rocky is inside his apartment, which is described as a drab, one-room apartment with a mattress that's used as a punching bag; but this description really doesn't give the flavor of the place that the film does. Rocky drops his coat on the floor, puts on a pair of glasses, and walks to the turtle bowl; however, he doesn't feed the turtles. He then returns to the kitchen, boils some water (a procedure that would take about three minutes), turns on the record player, picks up a hairbrush, and mimes the words to the song "All in the Game." Finally, he soaks his hand in the boiled water and the scene ends.

The only things in this scene remotely similar to the film version are the mattress that Rocky uses as a punching bag and the poster of Marciano. All he says to the turtles is, "Look who's home" (5B); there is no practicing of lines in the mirror; no reflecting on his life, past, present, or future; no photos of family, friends, or himself; and no allusions to religion. In short, there is nothing in the scene that is significant in either commenting on character or advancing story line in the same manner in which we see it in the final cut.

Scene 7
This "scene" is merely an establishing shot of the Philadelphia skyline at dawn, with the figure of William Penn rising above the city hall. In short, this shot has nothing to do with the scene to follow.

Scenes 8 and 9
These scenes take place at the dockyard. What's curious about these scenes is that there is no natural transition from Scene 7. It would have made more sense for the previous scene to be an establishing shot from the docks, creating a natural tie-in with the subsequent scenes. But as it's written, it has no apparent purpose other than to indicate the time of day.

Scene 8 opens somewhat the same way as in the film, but the dock-worker is named Fats, not Bob, and when he sees Rocky approaching, he doesn't make a run for it on his forklift, but rushes into a ship's hole. The content of the dialogue is basically the same as the film version, though more redundant, but the context is very different. As Fats offers Rocky his coat, Rocky grabs Fats' thumb and "bends him to his knees" (7A). Though Rocky doesn't break his thumb, he walks away saying, "That's what coulda' happened" (Stallone, 7A). This is a significant action because it shows us a completely different kind of Rocky. In the film, Rocky is compassionate. He gives back the coat, chastises the man for not paying his debts, and takes heat from Gazzo for not breaking Bob's thumb. In the script, he comes off as a thug, and even though he doesn't break Fats' thumb, he inflicts pain.

If the scene had remained as it was written, it would have run against the character grain. Recalling Aristotle's words about consistency, Rocky's character, to a great extent, must remain consistent. To be vicious in the ring is one thing; to be vicious outside the ring is something else. If the object of the scene is to connect the hero with the audience, Rocky cannot bend thumbs and inflict pain for profit. If the object of the scene is to alienate the audience, then Rocky can. Obviously, the former held out.

Scene 10

This is the initial scene outside the pet shop. Stallone writes that Rocky taps on the window and whistles. He sees a girl behind the counter and flattens his face against the window and at the same time does an impression of the Hunchback of Notre Dame. The girl is named Adrian Klein and is not "attractive, but pleasant-looking. Thirty years old. Brown hair pulled back. Light skinned. She wears glasses" (8).

We can overlook the fact that the name Adrian is a male name and Adrienne is a female name. But making faces like the Hunchback is a rather odd action and makes Rocky's character even less likable than he already is. When seeing his gesture in the window, Adrian wouldn't necessarily know it was supposed to be the Hunchback. In other words, she doesn't turn to the shop owner and say, "Look, Rocky's acting like Quasimodo again." Rather, someone might look at him and conclude that he's a bit mentally disturbed, and that's not the Rocky an audience would like and certainly not the Rocky that would attract Adrian. But Stallone doesn't stop there; inside the pet shop, Rocky gets worse.

Scene 11

This is a problematic scene because before Rocky begins talking about the turtle food, he assaults a female customer who's already purchased a puppy and put it into her "bag." Adrian asks the customer to remove the puppy and gets into a squabble with the customer, who claims she's paid for the puppy and can do anything she wants with it. At that point, Rocky snatches the bag out of her hand, takes the dog back, and gives it to Adrian. After Rocky reimburses the woman, the woman leaves. Then

Rocky begins with the turtle food dialogue. From that point on, the dialogue is basically the same as in the film, except for the ending of the scene, in which Rocky makes some rather irrelevant comments about the type of dog in the window. The store owner then sends Adrian downstairs to clean the cat cages and the scene ends with Rocky waving good-bye to Adrian and leaving the store.

Besides the fact that much of the store owner's dialogue seems irrelevant, if not incoherent, the scene closes in a completely different way than in the film. Rocky doesn't seem to mind that Adrian is sent downstairs to clean the cat cages and rather than close the scene with the allusion to "Crime doesn't pay," thus connecting to the subsequent scene, Rocky merely waves good-bye to Adrian and leaves.

So by the end of the same 10 percent of the script we're beginning to get a completely different image of Rocky than in the film version. In the script we have a character who is arrogant, who fraternizes with prostitutes, who assaults and intimidates women he doesn't even know. He is clearly not what Aristotle would call a likable character. In addition, in the script version, Stallone does little in the way of trying to create natural transitions between scenes, and the bum motif is entirely missing. In terms of trying to create a character an audience would like and relate to, Stallone misses the mark entirely by making Rocky somewhat nasty. He accents the fact Rocky is friendly with hookers, bends thumbs (but does not break them), and is rude to pet store customers. In fact, the original script creates Rocky as a completely different kind of person than he is in the film.

But the script actually gets worse. In Scene 80A, Rocky meets with then Philadelphia Mayor Frank Rizzo, who says that Rocky's been arrested nineteen times, been put on probation three times, and been expelled from seven schools (99A). In addition, the dialogue alludes to masturbation (Scene 15); has two characters cursing in Spanish (Scene 16); includes the phrase "Fuck you, creepo" (Scene 27), and has Gazzo turning Rocky's fight with Apollo into a race issue (Scene 51) when he says to Rocky, "We . . . gotta show these Afro-Americans where it's at."

All of these scenes have been eliminated primarily because they make Rocky out to be someone who the creative team must have felt was not in keeping with the kind of character it wanted. Someone, perhaps

Stallone, perhaps someone else, eventually revised Rocky's character to make him more compassionate and less crude and eliminated any allusions to racism, thus creating a character who would be more relatable to an audience.

If we return to Aristotle and recall what needs to be established during the first 10 percent of the script, we can see what was substantially revised in Rocky to accomplish those ends and how quickly it was done. The first seven scenes of Rocky, which effectively translates to about eleven pages of script (the rule being one page for every one minute of film time), and virtually thousands of dollars, take approximately eleven minutes of film time. As a matter of fact, the average Hollywood film today costs tens of thousands of dollars per minute, so you can see that there is absolutely no room for "cinematic fat" because film funders wouldn't tolerate that. Nor would Aristotle.

As I've discussed, the one similarity you'll find between scripts as seemingly dissimilar as Rocky and Kasdan's The Big Chill and Truffaut's Stolen Kisses and Henry's The Graduate is the approximate number of pages. At a minute per page, if the writer loses the audience in the first 10 percent of the script—or the first twelve to fifteen pages—the film will probably not get produced. There may be other reasons for that as well, but we're only dealing with the structure of the script at this point and not studio politics.

So, regardless of what has been written about screenwriting techniques, most scripts tend to follow a particular kind of structure, and someone, not necessarily Stallone, made Rocky work by following a structure. But how did he do that? The answer is that what any screenwriter is writing is a story, and unless the story is meant to be innovative, something that from the outset is meant to undermine the rules of storytelling and ignore the rules of time, character, and structure, then the story must adhere to certain prescribed limitations. Someone recognized the strong story and character potential in Rocky and suggested the character be altered to be more in tune with what an audience might relate to.

Unlike novelists, screenwriters are restricted by both time, fashion, and, most important, economics to create a product that will have a definite finishing time. By virtue of that finishing time, and a kind of contract with the audience that it will understand something about the story, it must also pay for itself by bringing in a certain amount of money. To that end, one is not only writing a screenplay; one may be writing a financial statement as well.

When *Rocky* opened in New York in November 1976, Vincent Canby (1976), the distinguished critic for the *New York Times*, called it a "sentimental little slum movie" (Canby, 288). But he also wrote that "throughout the movie we are asked to believe that Rocky is compassionate, interesting, even heroic, though the character we see is simply an unconvincing actor imitating a lug" (288). In contrast, for the then *Los Angeles Times* film critic Charles Champlin, "Rocky seems as brilliantly orchestrated as a fine if raucous symphony, alternating tumults and solitudes, humor . . . anger, small rejections and small victories, building to an ending which is surprising, ingenious, logical and blissfully pleasing" (1976, 67).

Apparently neither one of them ever read the script, though Champlin is closer to understanding the structure than Canby. According to Aristotle's tenets and the way the film version was produced, Rocky is compassionate, interesting, and, in a way, heroic. It's the script version that really makes him a lug and that was modified to make Rocky fit into a structure that would eventually meet with more audience approval than even Stallone could ever have imagined. I'll discuss how that was accomplished in the next chapter.

EXERCISE 1
Watch the first 10 percent of a standard feature film you have not seen before to see how quickly the main and supporting characters are introduced and how quickly the plot is established. In what order are the characters introduced? How long does it take to introduce those characters? In what way is the plot established? What elements are used to establish the plot and how does that relate to the overall structure? Finally, can you speculate, after viewing those ten to fifteen minutes, what the final outcome of the film may be? Use those markers in establishing a kind of foundation for your own screenplay.

EXERCISE 2
Watch a film and look for how many recognitions and reversals there are. When do they appear? How do they relate to the opening of the film? Do

they mark change? What kind of change do they mark? Does your script have the same kind of markers? If not, make sure you incorporate them.

WORKS CITED

Butcher, S. H., trans. 1951. *Aristotle's Theory of Poetry and Fine Art.* 4th ed. With critical notes. New York: Dover Publications.

Canby, Vincent. 1976. "Ringside Story." *New York Times* 22 November.

Carriere, Jean-Claude. 1994. *The Secret Language of Film.* New York: Random House.

Champlin, Charles. 1976. "*Rocky* Hits Right on the Button." *Los Angeles Times* Calendar Section, 28 November.

Rocky. 1976. Screenplay. Chartoff-Winkler Productions.

Sanders, Terry, and Frieda Lee Mock. 1981. *Word into Image: Portraits of American Screenwriters.* Santa Monica, CA: American Film Foundation.

2

The Hook, Its Arc, and the Question to Be Answered

NOW THAT WE'VE ESTABLISHED THE FUNDAMENTAL COMPONENTS of the Aristotelian script, we have to ask ourselves this question: What kind of opening did Stallone use to hook the audience? In a curious way, the origin of the word *hook* is the best point of departure because one of the definitions of a hook is "an angle," and we know that if one has a hook without an angle then one really doesn't have a hook. We also know that the function of a hook is to capture something. In our case, we can define a hook, then, as any compelling cinematic device that absorbs the reader's attention within the first few pages of a script, that establishes the beginning of both a character and a story line arc and posits a question to be answered. Let's take each of these items individually.

Perhaps the opening begins mysteriously, as in *Citizen Kane*, or in chaos, as in *Trainspotting*, or in introspection, as in *The Graduate*. The point is the opening should immediately make the reader forget the fact that she or he is reading a script. It should manipulate the reader into being absorbed by the telling of the tale. So one rubric we can come up with is this: "A script's success can often be measured by how well and how quickly it captures and maintains an audience's attention." For a screenwriter, this aspect is of critical importance because his first audience is not a viewer, but a reader; therefore, the writer must communicate exactly what she or he envisions in a way that will dramatically capture a reader's attention and allow that reader to visualize the story as it unfolds.

With that perspective in mind, I can suggest several types of openings, which include, but are not limited to, the following:

- openings of action
- openings of conscience
- openings of intrigue
- openings of humor

The three most recognized kinds of openings are:

- in the middle of the action
- on the threshold of the action, or the chronological beginning
- in a flashback

Within those categories we can find a number of other subcategories. For example:

- while the "crime"(sexual or otherwise) is taking place
- in the future; not of this time; an opening related to science fiction
- in the mind; introspection; openings that deal with a character's thoughts, often in voice-over
- in darkness; a state of doubt; openings that begin somewhat mysteriously; something that presents a warning or exposes something evil
- in the clouds; quirky, comical openings

These are merely examples of different types of openings. Obviously, they are not exhaustive, nor are they meant to tell you exactly how to open. They are merely suggestions to get you started. What you choose to open with is dependent on two things:

- how well the opening fits into the overall structure of the story
- how creatively you can imagine it

For example, gratuitous openings—unless intentionally ironic—will generally not work. That is, if the story is meant to be a drama about a father and his two young sons after the death of their wife and mother, then opening with a rollicking sex scene or a mafia massacre will probably seem gratuitous. Granted, it may be a good opening in terms of capturing the attention of a reader, but will it establish the arc of the entire piece and will it be able to contribute to answering the question to be answered? Equally as important, will it work?

The specific task of an opening is to present a scene or a series of scenes in which the *tenor* of the tale will be told, something that will immerse the reader immediately into the causation of the scene or scenes she or he is witnessing and expose the question to be answered. The opening, which we can also call the expository scene(s), will be responsible for initiating a number of features. It should:

- introduce the characters

- show some of their interrelationships

- establish the venue

- expose a conflict or complication, which will maintain itself for the greater part of the film, ultimately moving to the climax and dénouement

- present the question to be answered

For example, the initial seven scenes of the film version of *Rocky* clearly do those things. They establish an active opening (boxers boxing); introduce the main characters (Rocky and Adrian); establish the setting (South Philly); inject a complication (i.e., the bum motif); and initiate the beginning of both a character and a story arc; that is, it establishes a point of departure (Rocky is down and out), and by so doing, it establishes a point of destination (he will become something other than what he was).

The character arc, then, is that range of motion in the evolution of character from the point of departure to the point of destination. In other words, the story line must present a situation that will force the character to change or alter the circumstances of his or her character. The character arc also ties in with both the story arc—the circumstances that move the character through the change—and the question to be answered, which the story line implicitly poses at the opening of the script and which must be ultimately answered by the end of it. The film version of *Rocky* deals with that situation quite effectively; by the end of the film, the question initiated at the outset—Will Rocky remain a bum?—is answered at the end of the film: no.

You may be thinking perhaps only high-grade commercial films like *Rocky* have these components. So let's take two films totally different in form and substance from *Rocky* and see if they work as well: Herman Mankiewicz's *Citizen Kane* and Peter Greenaway's *The Cook, the Thief, His Wife, and Her Lover.*

The shooting script of *Citizen Kane* is dated July 16, 1940, and it was produced in 1941 with a running time of 119 minutes. The American film critic Pauline Kael suggests that, "the mystery in Kane is largely fake, and the Gothic-thriller atmosphere and the Rosebud gimmickry (though fun) are such obvious penny-dreadful popular theatrics that they're not so very different from the fake mysteries that Hearst's *American Weekly* used to whip up . . ." (Kael 1984, 5). Those comments may be true, but in the first 10 percent to 15 percent of the script, Mankiewicz has clearly structured an opening, which is tied into an arc that presents a question to be answered. It is curious to note that Mankiewicz did not originally write the script, but actually dictated it and in that sense was much like those singers of tales before him who had learned a particular method of storytelling, although formulaic, and were able to tell stories based on that formula.

The script is written in extreme detail, but we can summarize the opening scenes accordingly. Through a series of ten dissolves in the first thirteen scenes, the reader is moved from the confines outside Kane's palatial estate of Xanadu to inside Xanadu and specifically to Kane's bedroom. There is an increasingly deductive movement from a large landscape outside the confines of the estate to a narrower one within the estate, and the one main focus is a very tiny light that emanates from Kane's chambers.

As we get closer and closer to the light in the room, we see what Mankiewicz describes as the "literally incredible domain of Charles Foster Kane": the golf course, the zoo, the monkey terrace, the alligator pit, the lagoon, the great swimming pool, and so on. In Scene 13, Mankiewicz writes:

A snow scene. An incredible one. Big impossible flakes of snow, a too picturesque farmhouse and a snowman. The jingling of sleigh bells in the musical score now makes an ironic reference to Indian temple bells—the music freezes—

KANE'S OLD OLD VOICE: Rosebud! (Kael 1984, 96–97)

At approximately two minutes into the film, we hear the word *Rosebud*; at two and a half minutes, Kane is dead. For approximately the next ten minutes the *News on the March* segment follows. This is essentially divided into fifteen separate but integral components that summarize and highlight the entire story line that will follow:

1. Kane's funeral and Xanadu
2. history of Kane's newspaper empire
3. Kane's association with famous people
4. Kane's first news building
5. Kane's empire and its holdings
6. Kane's youth
7. Kane's association with Thatcher, his guardian
8. comments about Kane
9. Kane's marriage to Emily Norton
10. Kane's marriage to Susan Alexander
11. Kane's building of the Chicago Opera House
12. the constructing of Xanadu
13. Kane and politics
14. Kane and scandal
15. Kane's death

Mankiewicz has written a compelling hook, which intrigues as well as mystifies, and in the first two minutes has alluded to the question to be answered (QBA):

What is Rosebud?

This question is tied into a story arc, which is really a multiple one made of four individual arcs. Unlike Rocky, who begins in deprivation and attains a kind of hero-hood while following a single, sustained arc, we learn about Kane's character as he goes through an arc process that is mediated by the points of view of four different people, but which is still composed of one overriding arc. We meet Kane on his deathbed and move to how he got there, but not before the plot arc is summarized through the *News on the March* segment, which is a linear progression of events tracing Kane's life from 1895 to 1940 that summarizes his character arc from impoverished waif to financial tycoon.

Imbedded within the *News on the March* segment are a variety of scenes that comment on Kane's character and allude to the "secret of Rosebud." The clearest example of that is when Walter P. Thatcher recalls the journey he took to visit Kane's family in 1870 and is asked by someone in the room: "Is it not a fact that on that occasion the boy personally attacked you after striking you in the stomach with a sled?" (Kael 1984, 106). Clearly, if the question were irrelevant, Mankiewicz would not have included it.

At the conclusion of the *News on the March* segment, there is a scene in the projection room from which the newsreel has been screened, in which the word *Rosebud* not only is discussed by several shadowy reporters in the projection booth but becomes the primary focus of the scene. Even though there was no one in the room to hear Kane whisper, "Rosebud," we can suspend our disbelief long enough for the word to have significant importance not only in terms of establishing Kane's arc but also in initiating the question to be answered. At the end of that scene, Mankiewicz writes: "(NOTE: Now begins the story proper—the search by Thompson for the facts about Kane—his researches—his interviews with the people who knew Kane.)" (Kael 1984, 126). Thompson, a journalist, then begins a kind of quest (see Scene 4) to discover who Kane actually was.

It is not coincidental that by the time we get to Scene 116, which takes place in the interior of the Great Hall at Xanadu as all of Kane's worldly goods are being cataloged, the newspapermen in attendance begin discussing Kane's life, and the word *Rosebud* once again emerges, though by that time no one can still account for its meaning. In Scene 117, Mankiewicz writes, "Camera travels to the pile that he has indicated. It is mostly bits of broken packing cases, excelsior, etc. The sled is on top of the pile. As [the] camera comes close, it shows the faded rosebud and, though the letters are faded, unmistakably the word 'Rosebud' across it. The laborer drops his shovel, takes the sled in his hand and throws it into the furnace. The flames start to devour it" (Kael 1984, 294). Hence the QBA initiated at the outset is answered at the conclusion.

Mankiewicz has divided the story arc into four specific flashback segments, all of which comment on Kane through individual points of view as these characters reflect on their individual relationships with Kane:

Bernstein, his accountant; Leland, Kane's best friend and a drama critic; Susan Alexander, Kane's second wife; and Raymond, Kane's butler. Thompson interviews all four of them with one thing in mind: to discover what Rosebud is. In the process of trying to uncover that mystery, he learns a lot about Kane the man and the final comment about Rosebud comes from Thompson himself, who says, "Maybe Rosebud was something he couldn't get or something he lost, but it wouldn't have explained anything—Rosebud is just a piece in a jigsaw puzzle—a missing piece" (Kael 1984, 294). So even though Mankiewicz's script is dramatically and structurally superior to Stallone's, it still adheres to Aristotle's dictum that the end be linked to the beginning with inevitable certainty. The thread that keeps the entire script together is Thompson's quest to discover the meaning of Rosebud and through it we see how Kane's character arc has been shaped.

If *Citizen Kane* has an opening of mystery, then *The Cook, the Thief, His Wife and Her Lover* has a mixture of actions all happening *in medias res* and all keenly interdependent on a variety of images. For example, *The Cook, the Thief, His Wife and Her Lover* works on the levels of action and intrigue simultaneously. One cannot attempt to standardize these openings as if to say, "All films open in such and such a way." There are a number of variables at work, but these two films, produced over half a century apart, do have some things in common. The biggest item they have in common is running time: *Citizen Kane* is 119 minutes, *The Cook, the Thief, his Wife and Her Lover* is 126 so they each function within the parameters of constrained time and that constrained time will dictate just how much and how fast the expository information must be given. In each case the expository opening will immediately make a transition into the flow of the story line, which should be linked with the ending. The writer has only about ten to fifteen pages or ten to twenty pages of the script to establish the components addressed earlier.

One can't emphasize enough Aristotle's words about how the sequence of events is directed toward an end and the end is ineluctably connected with the beginning. It's practically impossible to write a script without knowing the ending. That's not to say one should know the exact way it will end in the final scene on the final page of the final script, but one should have an idea as to how the story will end. The details of the ending will become a matter of selection based on the structure and circumstances the writer has created and what the writer has done with the characters presented at the outset. We've seen the opening with Kane dying with the word *Rosebud* on his lips followed by a quasi-documentary of his life. If the word *Rosebud* weren't important, then Mankiewicz wouldn't have used it within the first two minutes of the film, but he knew in some integral way it was going to be linked with the ending.

As with *Citizen Kane*, one might suspect the opening of *The Cook, the Thief, His Wife and Her Lover* would suggest a question to be answered that would also be resolved by the conclusion of the film, and so it does. Greenaway opens *The Cook, the Thief, His Wife and Her Lover* in a dramatically compelling way. Greenaway's penchant for the artistic and dramatic, blended with long tracking shots, reflects his background in art history, but the film opens with what will become a kind of leitmotif: it opens with a pack of dogs scavenging for food. This opening immediately sets up a theme of the play: the act of eating, which plays a key role in the film. As the story begins, theatre curtains are opened by two ushers, revealing a scene with two trucks and one automobile, which comes screeching to a halt in front of a restaurant, La Hollandais, a name that suggests both food (hollandaise sauce) and Dutch art.

In a flurry of events, a man named Roy is dragged into the parking lot of a restaurant by several thugs, stripped naked, and forced by Spica (Michael Gambon) to eat dog excrement while Spica's wife, Georgina (Helen Mirren), casually smokes a cigarette in the backseat of their car. It is apparent that Spica is "the thief" and Georgina "his wife," and so two of the four principal characters have been presented within the first minute of the script.

As he forces Roy to eat the excrement, Georgina pleads with Spica to "leave him alone. Let's eat." But Spica isn't finished with Roy until he urinates on him and threatens to make him eat his own excrement after forcing it out his "cock, like toothpaste" all because Roy apparently owes him some money. Subsequent to assaulting Roy, Spica washes his hands in a bowl of water offered to him by an Asian woman who works in the kitchen of the restaurant. After insulting her, Spica pours the bowl into her face before taking Georgina in tow and, at the four-minute mark, walks into the kitchen of the restaurant. At this point we meet Richard (Richard

Bohringer), "the cook." Through the dialogue we discover that it's the restaurant's three-month anniversary and we learn that Spica and Richard are partners because the huge neon letters Spica's henchmen carry will eventually spell Spica & Boar's (though Richard's name is really Borst). But before the men set up the neon letters, we see that Spica's name is an anagram of the word *aspic*, which is a play on food because aspic is a kind of jelly composed of meat, fish, game, and eggs, and it is also a collateral of the word *spike*, which certainly resembles Spica's character.

So by the fourth minute of the script, three of the four characters have been introduced and, in the dialogue between Spica and Richard, a number of important story line components have been introduced. As Spica looks for something to eat from the menu (which indicates the day, Thursday), Richard names the French dishes in perfect French, because, of course, he's French, while Spica tries to repeat the same in Cockney, which emphasizes the vast cultural differences between them. When Spica mispronounces the word *poisson* as "poison," Georgina corrects him, only to be slapped in the face for her trouble. Clearly, the relationship between Georgina and Spica is based on both physical and verbal abuse, but just how much abuse and to what degree is not discovered until late in the film. It is also clear that Richard is the only character who can stand up to Spica with relative impunity, and he does not spare any sentiments he has for him. Finally, Spica walks out of the kitchen and into the dining room and after about 8 percent of the film has screened (or about ten minutes), Roy comes staggering into the kitchen, where Richard has him seated and hosed off as he offers him a glass of white wine.

After Spica and Georgina have entered the dining room proper, the camera passes by Michael (Alan Howard), "the lover," who sits alone, reading a book, at about the twelfth minute. At approximately minute 13, Michael captures Georgina's attention and the camera cuts back and forth between them several times within the same minute until Michael and Georgina actually see each other. At approximately the fifteenth minute, Michael goes to the bathroom and is joined by Georgina, and by the twenty-second minute they have returned to their respective tables. A few minutes later they return again to the bathroom and are having sex in one of the stalls when, a minute later, they are interrupted by Spica's entrance.

So a number of script components have already been established after about 10 percent of the film has aired:

- All four main characters have been introduced.
- The abusive relationship between Spica and Georgina has been established.
- The business relationship between Spica and Richard has been established.
- The potential sexual relationship between Georgina and Michael has been established.
- By virtue of those interrelationships, we see the beginnings of at least one character arc (Georgina's) as well as at least one question to be answered.

As with the previous scripts I've discussed, we can speculate that if the film begins with the thief doing something distasteful to someone else, by the end of the film, the thief should get a "taste of his own medicine," presenting both the initiation of an arc and a question to be answered:

Will Spica pay for what he does?

Likewise, we can speculate that for Spica to pay for what he does, there must be an alteration in Georgina's character from being victimized to being a victimizer. Since she is clearly the victim in an abusive relationship, another question to be answered might be:

Will Georgina be vindicated?

By the fifth day of Georgina's affair, Spica discovers that she has been cheating on him and, in a rage, vows to "kill him [Michael] and eat him." By the sixth day, Spica's men find Michael (who's been hiding from Spica in a book depository) and gruesomely murder him. When Georgina discovers the body, she is moved to ask for Richard's help in cooking Michael, thus fulfilling Spica's prophecy. Both questions to be answered are, in fact, resolved by the end of the film in very dramatic and interpenetrating ways. After Richard agrees to Georgina's plan, Richard closes the restaurant for a "private function" created especially for Spica, who shows up with only one of his henchmen, Mitchell (Tim Roth).

Georgina seats Spica at a table and after he's comfortable there's a grand entrance of all the people whom Spica has, during the course of the film, either humiliated, abused, or assaulted, led by Roy and Richard and several waiters who, like pallbearers, carry what we and Spica soon discover to be roasted Michael.

Georgina then unveils the cooked cadaver, as Spica looks on, horrified. Roy, who was introduced in the opening scenes of the film, pours Spica a glass of white wine, and in an ironic way, closes the circle begun when Spica urinated on him. Spica, sensing things are not going well, goes for his gun, which is quickly wrested from him and, through a change of hands, finally ends up in Georgina's. She points the pistol at Spica and commands him to eat, which, after vomiting, he painfully does. As Spica continues to chew a morsel of Georgina's dead lover, she takes aim and shoots Spica in the head. As he falls to the floor, the last word she utters is, "Cannibal," and the curtain falls on the play, thus answering both questions to be answered and, in effect, completing her character arc.

So we've seen in both *Kane* and *The Cook* that we have been dealing with hooks, character arcs, and, most important, questions to be answered: What is Rosebud? Will Spica pay for what he does? Will Georgina be vindicated? We see that in practically any standard feature film, if not most films, one can state a question to be answered at the outset and by the conclusion of the film, the question should theoretically be resolved.

But one can ask: What is the most effective way in terms of structure to resolve the question(s) to be answered? In Aristotle's word: *action*. We can think of the story line structure of the script in a way that is similar to character structure, that is, as an arc. In architectural terms, an arch is simply a form of construction in which a number of units span an opening by carrying the downward thrust laterally to the next unit and finally to the abutments or vertical supports. What we have here is a kind of cinematic arc, but it suggests the same thing.

The arc is separated into three divisions, with Act I and Act III more or less taking up an equal percentage of the arc and Act II taking up the majority of the arc. The arc is representative of the direction the story line takes. As the character goes through an arc from beginning to end, so too does the story line arc from the beginning to the end. Just as the arc of the character alters, so too does the story line alter.

Essentially, there is a combination of *action* and *alteration* that progresses in an elevated direction, peaks, and then declines, and within that action are three major components:

- setup: a situation to resolve and a question to answer
- development: a progression of the main situation and others
- resolution: an ending to the situation initially established that finally answers the question

As Aristotle has said, one has to consider the play as a whole—as a frame—which is set up in Act I, developed in Act II, and resolved in Act III. One must think of a script as a unified work with specific markers that register the beginning, middle, and ending, and the writer has to fit his or her idea within the boundaries of those markers. There has been a lot of controversy over just how many acts there are in a screenplay, and one can talk endlessly about a five-act scenario or even a nine-act scenario; one can start at the ending of the film and end at the beginning (e.g., *Citizen Kane*); but the fact of the matter remains that there must be a legitimate beginning that advances the thesis of the story, a middle that carries the action (regardless of the number of subplots incorporated), and a conclusion that will resolve the question(s) answered at the outset. It's that simple.

Like a formula novel, a feature screenplay is structurally rigid. One has a specific number of pages to work with, in this case, about 120 or within 4 percent to 6 percent of that mark in either direction. Because of that rigidity, there's absolutely no room for extraneous events, digressive and/or extended monologues or dialogues, superfluous action, or subplots in name only. In short, one must remember this rubric: anything that does not contribute to the linear flow of the story line, anything that does not propel the story forward, should be scrapped. Or, as Aristotle has said, if the presence or absence of something makes no apparent difference to the plot, it is not a real part of the whole and, therefore, it doesn't belong. So you can see how the question to be answered is integrally connected with the arc.

Once the QBA has been asked, the arc gives both character and plots a direction. If one wanted to look at how these three things fit together,

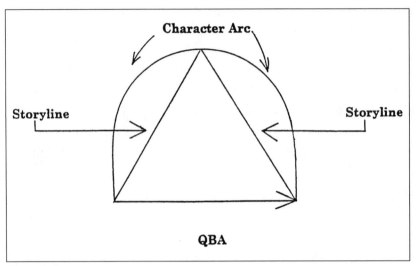

Figure 2–1.

one might use an equilateral arc, in which there is an overriding arc supported by an equilateral triangle (see Figure 2–1).

What's interesting about this particular type of arc is that if the over-riding arc represents the character arc, then two sides of the triangle can represent the story line supports to the character arc and the third side of the triangle can represent a kind of linear example of the question to be answered. In other words, the alteration in the main character is supported by the story line, which answers the QBA. We can apply that arc to filmwriting, so that we have something at the beginning of the film that relates to and unifies the ending. To return to *Rocky*, the film establishes that he is a down-and-out boxer and is considered by many to be a bum. The character arc, which is that movement that will unify the action, must alter that condition. The arc moves from his being a bum to his becoming a champion contender. If we take practically any film, we're going to see some kind of alteration in the protagonist contingent on some kind of problem or conflict. With that alteration there comes an implied arc, a range of action or movement that alters the nature of the protagonist and the direction of the story.

No one could imagine *Citizen Kane* and *The Cook, the Thief, His Wife and Her Lover* to be Hollywood-type films. Certainly Greenaway would broil and

Mankiewicz would have broiled at such a notion, yet in both of these films we do see similar components relative to both arcs and questions to be answered. But let's take a look at these components in an entirely different film, a purely Hollywood film: Barry Levinson's *Rain Man*, written by Academy Award winner Barry Morrow. We can take a look at segments of the opening and ending of this film to see if we can isolate the arcs and the question(s) to be answered.

The summary on the back of the *Rain Man* videocassette box says that Charlie Babbitt (Tom Cruise) is "a callous, self-centered young hustler . . . but what begins as an act of selfishness soon evolves into a mystical odyssey of camaraderie and self-revelation that expands the confines of Raymond's narrow world . . . and enables Charlie to grow beyond the limits of his hardened heart." To a great extent, this is true, but it's only one way of looking at the film. The opening hook is clear: Charlie Babbitt, "mid-twenties, with dark good looks and a restless intelligence behind the eyes," is in financial trouble (Morrow 1988, 1). We know from the opening scenes that he hustles Lamborghinis for big profits and, by the time the dialogue begins, we know that Charlie's got a financial crisis on his hands. At about minute 2, he says that he's got a "swing loan" outstanding for "two hundred thousand dollars," and if he doesn't get his money, the cars will be collected and he'll be finished. But we also discover that Charlie is not the type of person to take orders; rather, he's one to give them. As a matter of fact, Charlie cuts no slack for anyone, including his girlfriend, Susan, and his assistant, Lenny. He's short-tempered, arrogant, and self-indulgent—all the things necessary as a point of departure for a character to make a change by the ending.

After temporarily repairing his immediate financial problem, Charlie and Susan go on a trip to Palm Springs, leaving Lenny to handle the dirty work. During the drive she gets upset with him because he's so silent, to which Charlie responds by saying, "I'm glad your boss gave you Friday. Gives you three whole days to bitch at me." These characteristics are crucial to Charlie's personality and, before the first sequence of scenes is over—which in the script comes at page 8, but in the film at minute 6—both a character arc and a QBA are established. The immediate questions that are raised are:

Will Charlie continue to be self-absorbed?
and
Will Charlie solve his financial problems?

While Charlie and Susan are driving toward Palm Springs, Lenny calls Charlie on the mobile phone (at minute 6) to let him know that his father has died. The information barely affects Charlie emotionally, and he explains to Susan that the two of them were not very close; but the information enables both of them to fly from Los Angeles to Cincinnati for the funeral and the subsequent reading of the will. While Charlie is at his father's house, he recounts to Susan the reasons for the falling-out he had with his father, and as he rummages through his past at about the tenth minute, he recalls something about his childhood: a pretend friend named Rain Man, who would sing to him. So after ten minutes, almost the entire cast of main characters has been introduced: Charlie, Susan, and the Rain Man, if not in form, then in principle.

After the funeral, Charlie meets with his father's attorney, who tells him that he's not going to inherit anything but his father's prize roses and vintage Buick and that his father's estate has been put into a trust with a beneficiary whose name cannot be revealed. Upset that he won't collect a dime of the three million dollar inheritance, he deceives a bank official, who reveals the whereabouts of the person in charge of the trust. At approximately minute 16, Charlie meets Dr. Bruner, the administrator who runs Wallbrook, an institution for mentally retarded people. Dr. Bruner, who is also the trustee of the estate, gives Charlie minimal information about the trust and its beneficiary. At approximately minute 17, Charlie accidentally runs into Raymond (Dustin Hoffman), the autistic savant, who's outside looking at the '49 Buick that was bequeathed to Charlie by his father. Raymond appears to know everything about the car and to whom it belonged, which puzzles Charlie, and by minute 19 he discovers that Raymond is his brother. Given the fact that the entire film is 134 minutes long (from an original 159-page script), Raymond's entrance comes after approximately 14 percent of the film has aired, which is well within the prescribed standards. So, by the first 15 percent of the film, the entire cast of main characters has been physically introduced. At about minute 26 Charlie actually kidnaps Raymond as a way of getting even with his father for excluding him from his will, and they embark on a journey back to California.

While Charlie, Susan, and Raymond are spending the night in a local hotel suite, it's apparent that Charlie doesn't understand Raymond's temperament at all. He humiliates him, insults him, and treats him poorly. Susan appears to be the only person who understands, or attempts to understand, Raymond. Finally, fed up with the way Charlie deals with people, Susan leaves him at about minute 36. Charlie calls Bruner and demands half of the inheritance for Raymond's return but is denied. Not has he only kidnapped Raymond, but he's also holding him for ransom.

From that point on, the film focuses on the two brothers as they both separate from the mundane world and embark on a trip that will ultimately alter each of them to some degree. Because Raymond refuses to fly and makes a scene at the airport, they are forced to drive the Buick cross-country. Throughout their journey—from Ohio, to Missouri, to Texas, to New Mexico, to Nevada, to California—both of them must come to terms with each other, but the major portion of that responsibility belongs to Charlie. In other words, the trip becomes Charlie's quest. But there are also two major focal points that reappear throughout the film:

1. the allusions to Charlie's financial woes
2. the allusions to Raymond's ability with numbers

The first indication that Raymond has a special facility for numbers is the scene at minute 40 when, during their breakfast, the waitress drops a box of matches on the floor and Raymond knows exactly how many matches have spilled merely by glancing at them. This ability doesn't really affect Charlie, who's still preoccupied with getting his half of the inheritance.

As they continue to travel, Charlie begins to learn about Raymond's needs: where his bed needs to be; when his bedtime is; what he likes to eat, drink, and wear; all the things that remind Raymond of his routine at Wallbrook. These bits of minutiae tend to drive Charlie out of his mind. Fed up with Raymond's behavior, at about minute 60, Charlie finds a physician in a small town who attempts to explain Raymond's condition to Charlie, but he still doesn't seem to understand.

With the two of them in a motel at about minute 69, or approximately the midpoint of the film, Charlie has a number of revelations about Raymond. First, he discovers that Raymond is actually the Rain Man who used to sing the Beatles' "She Was Just Seventeen" to him. Second, while Charlie runs some bath water, Raymond starts screaming about "water burning the baby." Both of the these events appear to have a major impact on Charlie's behavior, so much so that after he puts Raymond to bed he calls Susan and apologizes. So we can see just how far his character has altered in the first 50 percent of the film.

They drive through Las Vegas, and stop outside of the city to have breakfast. While waiting for the meal, Raymond flips through the tabletop jukebox, and as he does, he recalls the names of the musicians and the numbers associated with the songs. Suddenly, something registers with Charlie. He mentions several musicians and Raymond responds with the appropriate jukebox number. Charlie then realizes Raymond's facility for remembering numbers and buys a deck of cards. At minute 84, Charlie tosses a number of cards to the ground and asks Raymond to tell him what's left in his hand. When Raymond tells him, Charlie realizes that Raymond can count cards without error and also realizes that he can use Raymond to his own ends, that is, to get out of debt.

They scramble back into the car and speed back to Vegas while Charlie explains the game of blackjack to Raymond. When they reach Vegas, Charlie pawns his watch and buys new clothes for Raymond to make him presentable. By minute 89, they enter the casino to play blackjack and, by minute 90, they've already won $85,000.

After a series of scenes that are meant to round out character and further establish a new kind of relationship between Charlie and Raymond (e.g., one in which Raymond is hustled by a hooker and one in which Charlie teaches him to dance), Susan shows up to tell him that she's unemployed because the business is over. The next day, when Charlie and Raymond return to the gaming tables, Charlie's invited to talk to security. Unbeknownst to Charlie, he was taped the day before and the head of security advises him that it would be best for him to take his winnings and leave, which the three of them do.

Once back in California, Charlie believes he can take care of Raymond by himself. He meets Dr. Bruner, who, as executor of the trust, offers him $250,000, but Charlie refuses the check, saying "it's not about money anymore." The next day, Raymond almost causes a fire in Charlie's house, which reinforces the fact that Charlie is incapable of taking care of

Raymond the way he needs to be taken care of. After a meeting with Raymond, Dr. Bruner, and a psychiatrist, it becomes clear to Charlie that the best thing for Raymond would be for him to return to Wallbrook. The film concludes with Charlie escorting Raymond to the train station to leave with Dr. Bruner.

In the penultimate scene, Charlie and Raymond sit with Dr. Bruner and a psychiatrist, during which time it becomes clear to Charlie that he cannot take care of Raymond the way he needs to be taken care of. After Dr. Bruner and the psychiatrist leave, Charley says that he likes having Raymond as a big brother, kisses his forehead, and stands by a window. In the closing scene, Raymond spells out Charlie's name and says, "My main man." In the final scene of the film, Raymond tells a joke that "Kmart sucks" and as Charlie leads him to the train for his trip back to Wallbrook, he tells him that he's packed the food he likes and that he'll visit him in two weeks. Raymond boards, and as the train leaves for Ohio, Charlie stands alone near the platform.

By the end of the film, Charlie's arc has been resolved and the QBA has been answered. To some degree, Charlie has changed, even though the change was rather precipitous. His character change really took place in about two days, since during the first part of their journey, Charlie was completely unsympathetic toward Raymond even though he knew he was his brother. But there has been a change. He has gone from being self-absorbed, stingy, and arrogant to being compromising and concerned for the welfare of his brother. And the QBA? Well, yes, he did solve his financial problems. Granted, he solved them by kidnapping his brother, holding him for ransom, and exploiting his skills, but his move was perfectly in line with the character that Morrow established at the outset. And even though by the end of the film, Charlie says it's not about money, he's already used Raymond, whom he once addressed as "the three million dollar man," to eliminate his debt.

Certainly Charlie has learned a lot of things from traveling with Raymond: consideration, moderation, and cooperation; but there can be no doubt that Charlie has also taken advantage of Raymond. The fact remains that Charlie's arc has been completed and the QBA has been answered by the end of the film, and to that extent, *Rain Man*, *Citizen Kane*, and *The Cook, the Thief, His Wife and Her Lover* have much more in common than approximate time length. We'll see more how these aspects relate in the chapter on quests.

EXERCISE #1

Pick a film, any film. After establishing its running time, watch 10 to 15 percent of the film and stop it. Then ask yourself the following questions and write the answers down:

1. How does the film open? What hooks has the writer used to capture your attention?

2. Is there a QBA? What do you think it is?

3. What do you think is the arc of the main character(s)? In other words, how do you think the character will change given what you've witnessed in the first 10 percent to 15 percent of the film?

After answering these questions, screen the remainder of the film to see if what you've suggested has actually been accomplished. Use this kind of an exercise to help structure your own script.

WORKS CITED

Greenaway, Peter. 1989. *The Cook, the Thief, His Wife and Her Lover.* Paris: Dis/Voir.

Kael, Pauline. 1984. *The Citizen Kane Book.* New York: Limelight Editions.

Morrow, Barry. 1988. *Rain Man.* Los Angeles: United Artists Pictures.

3
SCENE

Character, or Who Is This Hero Anyway?

TO A GREAT EXTENT, WE'VE BEEN DEALING WITH CHARACTER throughout the previous chapters, especially in terms of the arc and how the character must be altered by the conclusion of the film. But I can now begin to address specific things about character that I've not addressed yet. I'll begin by answering this compelling question: Are film characters real? If yes, why? If not, why not? One is apt to say, logically, that of course they are real. What else could they be? But in fact, at least in cinema fact, they're not real, they're cinelogues. A cinelogue is a character who is real only by virtue of the fact that she or he exists on the screen. Nothing more, nothing less. And even if the script is a biopic, what you see on the screen is nothing more than a cinelogue, a measure of who that person may have been in real life, but really a measure of someone else's imagination realized on film. Butch and Sundance were not handsome men, neither was Clyde, and Bonnie did not look like Faye Dunaway, nor did Jimmy Smits look like Arroyo in The Old Gringo. Enough said about reality. As with film dialogue, what we're dealing with in terms of character is not character as such, but character as simulacrum, an image or a semblance of something real. We know there's too much complexity in any human being to reduce him or her to two finely edited hours on the big or a small screen. Even in Rocky's situation, I've avoided talking about a number of things relating to his character and economic situation such as: Where are his parents? What kind of upbringing did he have? What psychological ramifications affected him? Was he an abused child? How did he get in the position he's in? Did he have any employment before being a thug? When did he lose his virginity? With whom? How long has he been courting Adrian? And most important . . . are those his original goldfish? And on and on. As a screenwriter you must create characters—especially heroes—that appear real to the point that an audience can relate to them, and simplifying the complexity of any one individual character achieves that mission.

The failure of many film characters is that the screenwriter tries to make them too complex and in the face of that daunting task tends to lose the relative simplicity of the character. The writer attempts to make them appear more like real humans instead of fictional ones, or of cinelogues. That may sound rather callous, but realistically there's not a lot you can do in two hours of real time, not to mention the fact that once the script has left your hands it will inevitably be altered by anyone who has the physical ability to turn a page.

Even in a film as genuinely pleasing to some people as *Life Is Beautiful*, the audience knows little about the character of Guido (Roberto Benigni) prior to the time he is introduced. We know nothing about how he genuinely feels emotionally or psychologically, about surviving in a concentration camp, since most of his attention is taken with securing the safety of his son. He never shares that experience with any of the other inmates and his comic antics, which realistically would have resulted in immediate extermination, only preclude any serious consideration of what a human being in that situation may have truly felt.

So what can you do, as a screenwriter, in relation to developing character? In other words, what are your goals in creating character? Actually, it comes down to two very specific things:

1. focusing on the conception of character(s)
2. focusing on the presentation of your character(s)

But how does one conceive a character, and what do I mean by presentation? I've already discussed character arcs and how there must be an alteration in the protagonist's character from the outset of the film to its conclusion, but you must also create a contrast between and among the characters. In other words, in the process of character conception, you need to individualize the characters, which is achieved through establishing differences between and among them. For example, in the film

Heat, the characters played by Robert DeNiro and Al Pacino, the "bad" criminal and the "good" cop, actually learn something from each other, and their individual arcs alter by virtue of the fact that though they are contrasted with each other, some significant similarities bind the two together, so much so that the last scene of the film has Pacino holding DeNiro's hand after he's mortally shot him.

So what differences might you look for in an attempt to individualize character? In other words, what components can you create to make your characters appear realistic? First, you have to think about your character's life. What makes any character an individual? What idiosyncrasies does he or she have that individualize him or her? What traits can you think of that will make a particular character memorable? There are certain key items you should keep in mind in conceiving character, which include, but are not limited to, the following:

- the physical
- the dictional
- the motivational
- the historical
- the relational
- the psychological

We can take a look at each of these categories one at a time.

Physical. Examples of this kind can include, but are not limited to, characters that have a physical deformity, a disability, or a disease. Such examples include Mel Gibson in *The Man Without a Face*; John Hurt in *Elephant Man*; John Voight in *Coming Home*; Marli Matlin in *Children of a Lesser God*; Jack Nicholson in *As Good as It Gets*; Dustin Hoffman in *Midnight Cowboy* and in *Rain Man*.

The character may have an addiction, as in *Trainspotting*, or a debilitating or fatal disease, as in *Philadelphia*, *Lorenzo's Oil*, or *Bang the Drum Slowly*. What is important in this case is that the main character or adjunct characters must somehow recognize, overcome, or cope with the situation rendered to him or her. Not only does that reason for being give a character a sense of individuality, but it should also work in conjunction with the storyline you've invented.

Dictional. The character could have a dictional component in his or her personality, as in the use of vocal rhythm or intonation or the repetitive use of a word or phrase. Examples include, Rocky's repetitive use of "Yo!" or "Absolutely," Ratso Rizzo's nasal intonation, the Rain Man's monotone voice, and Forrest Gump's twang. It could be Dennis Christopher's obsession with speaking Italian in *Breaking Away* or Robin Williams' tendency to lapse into one of his stand-up comedy routines in films like *Mrs. Doubtfire*, *Toys*, and *Dead Poet's Society*. These dictional qualities tend to individualize a character and can create a memorable character.

Likewise, you can stress an individual's vocal milieu. In other words, the use of an accent becomes an important character tool. Does your character come from the deep South? The heart of the Midwest? The ranges of the Southwest? The urban Northeast? Those vocal qualities can contribute to expanding and rounding out character.

Motivational. What motivates a character? What is it that makes this character do what she or he feels compelled to do? What motivates Rocky to want to go the distance? What compels Indiana Jones or James Bond or Batman to constantly risk his life? What causes Lester Birnham in *American Beauty* to alter his behavior? These become the circumstances that make up the fabric of the film. If Rocky didn't care if people thought he was a bum; if James Bond could care less about nuclear proliferation; if Benjamin didn't want to have sex with Mrs. Robinson; if William Wallace didn't want to seek revenge on the English; or if Lester Birnham were satisfied with his middle-class life, what would we be left with?

Motivation becomes a driving force in individualizing a particular character. With it, one can create numerous situations for the character to overcome; without it, there's not a lot for the character to accomplish. That motivation becomes part of the character's personality. Whether it is the will to succeed, the will to win, the will to power, or the will to change, what motivates an individual character becomes a part of who that character is.

Historical. The Backstory. Where does this character come from? How does the environment play a role in the character's personality? Is the character's family important? And how might that affect his or her character? How does the character function on the job? We understand Rocky's job and how well he does it in the first eleven minutes. We also find out a bit about Rocky and Adrian's history—their backstory—when he and Adrian are ice-skating.

We find out why Parry (Robin Williams), in *The Fisher King*, is living beneath the streets of Manhattan when Jack Lucas (Jeff Bridges) tries to find him. We discover the backstory of Adso (Christian Slater) in *The Name of the Rose* during the monologue and after he arrives at the monastery.

Somewhere in the course of the script and, generally, early the first act, the reader needs to get some obligatory information that will tell him something about the character's history in order for him to understand more about the character's present. To do that, one needs to create scenes in which this information is presented in a way that appears normal, not contrived.

Relational. What's the individual's marital status? Sexual preference? Family life? Are there siblings? Friends? Does the character have a buddy? A confidante? Think about buddies in relation to story line. We know of numerous buddy pictures with partners such as Gibson and Glover or Thelma and Louise or Butch and Sundance, or people in whom the main character trusts as buddies as in *Forrest Gump* or *Ghost*. It does not necessarily need to be a partnership, but a relationship in which the buddy may also turn out to be a mentor of sorts.

One needs to explore relations between and among characters in situations outside of the workplace. Where does the character hang out? What does the character do in those situations with other people? How does he relate to others? We see that Rocky frequents a particular tavern, that he has a volatile relationship with his boss' driver, and that he tries to be a role model for kids in the neighborhood. In *Rain Man* we see what kind of relationship Charlie Babbitt has with his girlfriend and with those who work for him, and each of those relationships offers an opportunity for you to explore something else about a protagonist's character.

Psychological. What does the character do when alone? How does the character react to certain events or situations? This is an extremely important point and can't be overlooked because of the powerful nonverbal possibilities as well as the dialogous ones. One of the best examples of how the psychological operates is in *Ordinary People*, in which, during the course of the film, Conrad explores the psychological demons that haunt him. It is during that exploration that his character can rid himself of the demons and resolve his situation. In *Heat*, DeNiro's character believes fully in the aphorism that when the heat is present, one must make a decision in thirty seconds to fight or flee and that aphorism plays a major role in his psychological behavior not only with Pacino's character but with the woman he presumably loves. In *American Beauty*, Lester Birnham must somehow reconcile his psychological fantasies about having sex with his daughter's teenage friend and the reality of actually attempting it.

Obviously, these are only a handful of possibilities, but they all help round out a character and contribute to an understanding of the character's past and present. These are only several examples you can think about in conceiving and presenting a character, but they all contribute to differences and because of these differences between and among characters, the characters relate differently to one another. Failure to contrast characters and develop relationships between them is one of the most common problems of novice scripts. For example, we know that Rocky loves Adrian; tolerates Adrian's brother, Paulie; both loves and hates Mickey; and idolizes Apollo. We know that Conrad does not get along with his mother; relates somewhat to his father; and will eventually connect with Berger in a way that is more personal than that of his parents. Lester Birnham has fallen out of love with his wife; has a miserable relationship with his daughter; and valorizes the kid next door who sells him drugs. These contrasts help round out each character and make characters give the appearance of being lifelike even though we know they're cinelogues.

But what do I mean by round character? I borrow the term *round character* from E. M. Forster's book *Aspects of the Novel*, in which he writes, "The test of a round character is whether it is capable of surprising in a convincing way" (1955, 78).

To round out characters, you need to create situations for them to act out and say things—action and dialogue—that are in keeping with their characters even if they are surprising. One of the biggest failures in character creation is making a cinelogue go out of character after you've worked so hard to get it in character. A prime example of this is the scene in *Rocky* in which Adrian virtually changes from the homely, self-effacing pet store clerk to a fashionable beauty, complete with makeup and coiffeur, after only a few trysts with Rocky. A surprise? Yes. A convincing surprise? No. Stallone (or someone else) went to great lengths to make her character very self-conscious about her appearance and did a fairly consistent job with her character in getting her finally to stand up to her brother and fend for herself; but her character, realistically, is still one that's terribly self-conscious and lacks a lot of self-confidence. When she loses her virginity and changes in terms of her sensuality, she is not convincing but merely becomes a cliché. Clearly, the experience had little or no effect on Rocky's character. In other words, having sex with Adrian didn't alter his dressing habits to the same degree, nor did he begin wearing cologne.

To that end, I need to note that in order to round out characters, the writer needs to have them interact with one another and with themselves on several levels:

1. They will express conflict in quest of their desires.

Rocky's desire is wanting to go the distance; he wants to prove to himself and to others he's not a bum, but in so doing he goes through a number of battles both small and large before he can win the war. Dave Stoller (Dennis Christopher), in *Breaking Away*, has conflicts between being who he is, the son of a blue-collar worker from a tiny town in Indiana, and who he is not, a bike rider who fashions himself Italian in body and spirit. The entire cast of *The Big Chill* seem to be in conflict with their pasts.

Because in any feature film there must be the infusion of conflict in order to destabilize the status quo and instigate the protagonist to action, it becomes easier to create hazards to initiate that conflict, which, at the same time, will also contribute to rounding out the character.

As I've indicated, in many ways what I'm talking about relates to the quest again: Rocky's quest in the *Rocky* films; Indiana Jones' quest in the *Indiana Jones* films; Richard Dreyfuss' quest in *Close Encounters*; Benjamin's quest in *The Graduate*; Conrad's quest in *Ordinary People*; both Joe Buck's and Ratso Rizzo's quests in *Midnight Cowboy*; Adso's quest in *The Name of the Rose*; Thelma and Louise's quest in the movie of the same name. In each of these films, hazards, obstacles, and obstructions, both psychological and physical, have been set up for the protagonists to overcome, and in overcoming them, the character becomes a more well-rounded person as he or she quests for his or her desire.

2. They interact in either communicative or antagonistic ways.

In an attempt to round out characters, one has to decide how they interrelate and how that interrelationship is revealed through social intercourse. Rocky and Adrian, Rocky and Apollo, Rocky and Mickey, Rocky and Gazzo's chauffeur all interrelate in different ways and in that difference lies much of who they are as characters. How Charlie Babbitt in *Rain Man* relates to Raymond at the outset of the film alters significantly by the end of the film, and in each individual encounter Charlie has with Raymond, there is something to say about his character. Early on, he's not at all interested in communicating or understanding Raymond or Raymond's behavior and to that end, he's clearly antagonistic, only concerned with exhibiting his narcissistic attitude. But by the end of the film, it would appear that he has learned how to communicate and, in great measure, how to love. Charlie Babbitt, like Adrian, is a clear example of a cinelogue because his enormous change in character happens in less than a week. Granted, living with someone like Raymond might significantly change a person, but for that alteration to occur in that short of a time is highly unlikely; one must therefore attribute that "deceit" to the skill of screenwriters who have condensed a kind of behavior that should have taken a significant amount of time to develop into a rather insignificant amount of time without drawing attention to that fact. The object here is to create characters whose differences not only define who they are but who they are not and decide how those differences affect will affect their inter-relationships.

3. *They view their situations with a prevailing point of view.*
In other words, characters tend to view particular situations from a specific viewpoint, a particular worldview. If Rocky believes he's a bum, he will tend to look at every situation from that point of view. If Charlie Babbitt is selfish, his actions will be predicated on that selfishness. If Jack Lucas, in *The Fisher King*, is totally preoccupied with himself, his actions will be predicated on that egocentricity.

By knowing a character's particular worldview, you will know how that character will react in a given situation. How is a character's worldview reflected in what the character does or says? If one is a member of an oppressed minority, as in *The Color Purple*; if one eventually discovers that the present has nothing to do with the past, as in *The Big Chill*; if one believes that in spite of any hardship, one can achieve anything, as in *Rocky* or practically any Disney feature; or if one believes that regardless of one's status, love can conquer all, as in *Il Postino*, it will be evinced in dialogue and action, both of which constitute a character's worldview.

However, since the characters must alter during the course of the film, you must alter their attitudes and at the same time alter the audience's appreciation of that alteration so that eventually Rocky doesn't think of himself as a bum, but as a champion; Conrad comes to terms with his guilt; Benjamin takes responsibility for his actions; Charlie Babbitt learns to be considerate of others; and so on. And that is not easy to do.

I've given examples on how to create character and present character to make cinelogues appear realistic; now I will utilize what I've been talking about by discussing several films:

Breaking Away, by Steve Tesich (Academy Award, Best Original Screenplay, '79)

Rocky, by Sylvester Stallone (nominated for Academy Award, Best Original Screenplay, '76)

Ordinary People, by Alvin Sargent (Academy Award, Best Adaptation, '80)

The Big Chill, by Barbara Benedek and Lawrence Kasdan (nominated for Academy Award, Best Original Screenplay, '83)

In this group, there is one major ensemble film, *The Big Chill*, with eight characters, and three character-driven pieces, one of which could be considered a minor ensemble film, *Breaking Away*, with four characters. Let's take each film separately and look at how the writers have conceived and presented their characters, keeping in mind the following:

physical
dictional
motivational
historical
relational
psychological

BREAKING AWAY
Opening Quarry Scene
Breaking Away is a minor ensemble film. A minor ensemble film would

deal with no fewer than three or more than four main characters. What brings the four adolescents together is that they are all cutters, a nickname given to those people who are native to Bloomington, Indiana. The word comes from the fact that the largest employer in the town, Indiana University, was essentially built by men who cut limestone. It is a pejorative term generally applied to the locals by the university students who are merely temporary residents. But each character has individuality that surfaces in relation to the others, and their individuality tends to contrast them. The main characters are:

Cyril, the comic/self-deprecator
Mike, the rebellious leader
Moocher, the angry little man
Dave, the romantic

Though the film is really about Dave, because it specifically follows his quest, each character shares something in common in that they are all in the process of growing away from one another, breaking away from the past. During the course of the film, each one comes to terms with his own individuality, which often results in conflict because they are all at a point in their lives when doing everything together as they once did is no longer appealing. Cyril begins as someone without direction; he ends by taking the SAT. Mike begins as a somewhat embittered young man envious of the college boys but takes pride in the fact he's the leader of the group; he ends by being somewhat less embittered but no longer the leader of the pack. Moocher begins as one of the guys; he ends by being the first to get married. Dave begins without an interest in higher education and enamored of things Italian, but he soon gets trapped in his own delusions; he ends by realizing the error of his ways and finally goes off to college.

Probably the best example of this division occurs as early as page 1 of the script, with the four of them walking toward the quarry. The dialogue clearly individuates each of the characters:

MIKE: I sent away for this stuff from Wyoming. It'll tell you everything. Since you don't believe me maybe you'll believe it when you see it.
CYRIL: And we'd work on the same ranch and sleep in the bunkhouse together, eh?
MOOCHER: That's the whole point.

CYRIL: I always miss the whole point.

MOOCHER: It'd be nice to have a paying job again, that's for sure.

DAVE: Niente laborare. Niente mangare.

MIKE: What's that mean?

DAVE: You don't work. You don't eat.

CYRIL: That's a terrible thing to say. Are you really going to shave your legs?

DAVE: Certo. All the Italians do it.

MIKE: That's some country. The women don't shave theirs.

CYRIL: STOP! [Pauses as if thunderstuck; hand on heart] It was somewhere
    along here that I lost all interest in life. Ah, right over there. I saw Dolores
    Reineke and fat Marvin. Why? Why Dolores?

MOOCHER: They're married now.

MIKE: You see what I saved you from, Cyril. Had I not told you about the two of
    them you never would have followed them out here.

CYRIL: Thank you, Mike. You made me lose all interest in life and I'm grateful.

MIKE: My brother says he saw you and Nancy. Moocher.

MOOCHER: When?

MIKE: Last Friday?

MOOCHER: Wasn't me. I'm not seeing her anymore. (Tesich 1978, 1–3)

It's clear from the dialogue that the characters are not only becoming individualized, but each of them is on a kind of individual quest (this film coalesces comedy, romance, and quest), which is ultimately satisfied by the end of the film. Mike takes the lead in almost everything—he wrote to Wyoming about the ranch, he informed Cyril about Dolores, he has a comment about Dave's legs, he tells Moocher about Nancy. Dave responds to almost everything with an Italian flair. Moocher, who says he's not seeing Nancy, actually is. Cyril is the group clown. But in terms of character arc, there is one overriding arc, Dave's, and three minor arcs that intersect the major arc, and each one of the four characters learns something about Dave by the end of the film.

ROCKY
Ice-Skating Scene
This obligatory scene has some significant historical information not only about Rocky but about Adrian as well, and the information becomes important in shaping who these characters have become. From the previous scene we know that for Adrian, it's Thanksgiving Day, but for Rocky it's just another Thursday, which says something about the relationship

between Rocky his family, but it doesn't say enough. For example, are his parents dead or does he not have a relationship with them? Do his parents live far away, causing a separation, or is there something else that has split them? These questions are raised, but not answered. They tend to shroud Rocky in a kind of mystery, but that mystery is marginally essential to his character.

The skating scene itself establishes the contrast between Rocky and Adrian and shows how, in some way, they are meant to be together because they are marginal characters living in a kind of marginal world. It unites the intellect with the brute. She is not yet, but will become, the Beauty to Stallone's Beast, and she will become that beauty by virtue of Rocky's love for her.

ADRIAN: Aren't you skating?
ROCKY: Ain't skated since I was fifteen—that's when I started fightin'—gotta watch the ankles. Yeah, fightin' use to be tops with me, but no more. All I wanted to prove was I weren't no bum—that I had the stuff to make a good pro.
ADRIAN: And you never got the chance?
CLEANER: Nine minutes!
ROCKY: Hey, I ain't cryin' . . . I still fight. Kinda do it like a hobby. See I'm a natural southpaw an' most pugs won't fight a southpaw 'cause we mess up their timin' an' look awkward, nobody wants to look awkward—southpaw means lefthanded . . . But I guess in the long run things probably worked out for the best, right? (Stallone 1976, 44–45)

Later in the same scene . . .
ROCKY: Yeah—my ol' man who was never the sharpest told me—I weren't born with much brain so I better use my body.
[For the first time, Adrian laughs.]
ROCKY: [Continuing] What's funny?
ADRIAN: My mother told me just the opposite. She said, "You weren't born with much of a body so you'd better develop your brain." (46)

Though the script has been slightly modified in the film, what's clear is that the scene gives us some additional information about the characters that will be critical to the story line; specifically, we learn that Rocky is a southpaw and that peculiarity makes the way he fights against his opponents—and, by extension, Apollo—significant. We learn that Rocky's father told him he wasn't very smart so he should use his body; Adrian counters with her mother telling her she didn't have much of a body, so she should use her brains. We also get the reprise of the bum motif that is established in the first scene and is repeated throughout the film until the night before the championship fight when he expresses his desire "to go the distance" to Adrian.

This shows how important it is to structure some kind of obligatory scene in which historical information can be given and in which you can isolate particular characters in order to give a better sense of who they are.

ORDINARY PEOPLE
Breakfast Scene

This scene is an excellent example of clarifying character and of contrasting the characters both relationally and psychologically. Not only does the scene imply certain things, but the physical placement of the characters is also important. The first thing one notices is the placement of the plates and juice glasses at breakfast. Not only is the placement fastidious in its organization, but the dishes are arranged in a triangle, and triangles can often imply conflict.

After Conrad (Timothy Hutton) comes down to breakfast, both he and his father, Calvin (Donald Sutherland), sit next to each other while Conrad's mother (Mary Tyler Moore) remains detached, standing at the sink, a relationship that acts as a leitmotiv throughout the film. The father is constantly concerned about his son's welfare and the mother remains physically and emotionally detached. She appears to have no time either to talk or to eat, even though she's set a place for herself.

CALVIN: [With gusto] Here he is.
CONRAD: Morning.
BETH: [Big smile] 'Morning.
CALVIN: Did you sleep well?
CONRAD: [Energetic] Yeah.
CALVIN: Hungry?
CONRAD: Hungry? . . . Uhm . . .
[Beth is putting French toast in front of Conrad. He looks at the plate.]
BETH: It's French toast.
CONRAD: Uh-huh.
BETH: It's your favorite.
CALVIN: Breakfast, pal, remember? Main meal? Energy? C'mon get some
    pounds on.

CONRAD: Why? I'm in chorus.
CALVIN: You're a swimmer.
CONRAD: Yeah . . . [Shrugs] . . . But I'm not hungry.
BETH: If you're not hungry, you're not hungry . . .
[Beth takes the plate and moves to the sink with it.]
CALVIN: Wait a minute, he'll eat it. [Big grin] Con! It's French toast!
[Beth scrapes the toast into the garbage disposal.]
BETH: There's fresh fruit for you when you get home from school, Conrad.
[She turns on the disposal.]
CALVIN: [Big grin] What are you doing?
BETH: Can't save French toast. [Looks at clock] Uh oh, I have to go. We're play-
    ing at nine.
[She reaches over and turns off the disposal.]
BETH: Honey, would you call Mr. Hermann about the shutters? I can't get any-
    where with him.
[She exits.]
CALVIN: [Calls after her] You have to charm Mr. Hermann. Did you charm him?
    [To Conrad] She never likes to charm Mr. Hermann. (Sargent 1979, 11–12)

It's also apparent that she never likes to charm her son either. We see that when Conrad says he's not hungry, Beth immediately removes the French toast from the table and, disregarding the protestations of her husband, stuffs it in the garbage disposal. Then she walks out of the kitchen, asking her husband to take care of some domestic business she'd rather not deal with. The husband's intervention is merely met with yet another kind of indifference. Her lack of a response to his comment "Did you charm him?" clearly reinforces the kind of character she is.

After she leaves, Calvin is the one who voices his concern for his son, a concern that Conrad is not yet willing to accept. When Conrad mentions that some friends are picking him up, his father suggests that they come over and play touch football since "he doesn't see much of the old gang anymore." The reason for that is because the friends are friends of Conrad's older brother, whom we discover has drowned in a boating accident. As Conrad gets up to leave, carrying a copy of Hardy's *Jude the Obscure* (a novel that deals with, among other things, crushed aspirations) in hand, he does not respond to his father's suggestion, thus distancing himself from the only parent who is genuinely concerned about his welfare.

The scene brilliantly explores in a very insightful way the interrelationships between and among the three main characters by establishing who they are, what their interests are, how they relate to one another, and what they think of themselves. In short, the scene is a remarkable one in individualizing character.

THE BIG CHILL
Opening Sequence

Finally, we come to *The Big Chill*. This is a major ensemble film with eight characters—nine if you count the dead Alex—all of whom are brought together because they had (*had* being the operative word) one major thing in common: they all either attended college at the University of Michigan or knew the deceased, Alex. Beyond that, time and circumstance have altered their characters and the writer has to make accommodations for that alteration. But the opening sequence that presents the characters (which is very similar to the French film *Le Grand Bouffe*) is an excellent way of individualizing character because from the very outset, and in a nonverbal way, we find out a great deal about who these people are, what they do, and, by extension, their attitudes toward certain things.

In the first three pages of the script, Kasdan and Benedek go into minute detail about how the sequence should be presented. Without going into the entire description, I'll take a look at these characters individually and see how they are shaped. As the film opens, we see:

HAROLD and SARAH: This is the typical upper middle-class family; Sarah (whom we discover is a physician) is on the phone, while her husband, Harold, is bathing the toddler. They are children of the 60s as witnessed by the fact that dad has already taught their junior how to sing Three Dog Night's lyrics to Jeremiah Was A Bullfrog. The fact that Sarah has received bad news is clear by the expression on her face. As the script reads: "After several long moments, Sarah appears in the door of the bathroom and leans against the doorjamb. Very quietly she is crying. Harold looks up at his wife" (Kasdan 1).

We now begin the series of "intercuts" with both Alex and the other characters that will, in an immediate way, shape who and what they are.

ALEX GETTING DRESSED I: (All Extreme Close-ups) "A suit pant leg, neatly pressed, pulled over a tanned calf" (Kasdan 1).

KAREN: She's the dutiful housewife sitting alone in her state-of-the-art kitchen, dressed in her designer tennis outfit, contemplating the sadness around her.

The script reads "a lavishly and recently remodeled kitchen, all dark-grained cabinets and gleaming tiles" (Kasdan 1).

ALEX GETTING DRESSED II: "A crisply starched shirt gets buttoned up the chest by strong male fingers" (Kasdan 2).

MICHAEL: He's the journalist; surrounded by books, he is also a bit 'spacey' as he can't seem to find what he's actually looking for until his partner finds it for him. The script reads: "Very calmly, she extracts a new package of batteries from the debris of the desk and places them in Michael's hand. . . . He enfolds her in his arms, sadly. She soothes him" (Kasdan 2).

ALEX GETTING DRESSED III: "The shiny buckle of a dress belt is fastened over the buttons of the suit pants" (Kasdan 2).

MEG: Is an attorney and from the looks of her office, with its corner penthouse view, she appears to be successful, at least in terms of her profession. The script reads: "then (she) lights up a cigarette and stands gazing over the briefcase at the Atlanta skyline." (Kasdan 2).

ALEX GETTING DRESSED IV: "A shiny black oxford is tightly knotted on a black-stockinged foot. A man's finger rubs a single scuff" (Kasdan 2).

SAM: He, a television actor, appears to have affinity for women and alcohol. As we see him in the first-class section of an airplane, he's obviously finished four bottles of what appears to be gin or vodka and the flight attendant "reveals the cover of the top magazine with a flourish: it is US *Magazine* and on the cover is a smiling-shot of Sam" (Kasdan 2). But before he autographs it he holds up an empty bottle of alcohol and shakes it as way of asking for yet one more.

ALEX GETTING DRESSED V: "A woman's sleek fingers have made a neat knot in a conservative tie. Now they slide the knot lovingly, almost sensually, up to the collar" (Kasdan 3).

CHLOE: Is the young, twentysomething, nubile, new age, bohemian and as such tells us something about the kind of woman Alex liked. The script reads: "Her long, wonderful, generous body is bent at an impossible angle. She is working hard" (Kasdan 3).

ALEX GETTING DRESSED VI: "A brush pulls his thick hair neatly away from a part. One more touch makes it perfect" (Kasdan 3).

NICK: Is flaky, a procrastinator, possibly drug dependent, and, as we'll discover, is the closest thing we have to Alex himself. As Nick drives his fading 911 we see a hand open the glove compartment, reach for a bottle of pills, flip off the cap, and shake them into the passenger's seat. The script reads: "The fingers forage through pills, picking out only white ones." (Kasdan 3). Not so coincidentally, the implication is that Nick has swallowed the pills and the next shot has the 911 "speeding" away.

ALEX GETTING DRESSED VII: This is the last of the Alex intercuts and the one that makes the final comment since the script reads: "the fingers pull the cuffs down, to cover that which body make-up could not hide—the straight, awful slits across the tender insides of the wrists" (Kasdan 3).

ALEX: Well, Alex is dead, but he's made his appearance through this brilliantly edited series of intercuts as the other characters are introduced. It is only in the final shot that we realize he's actually in a mortuary because he has committed suicide and that his death is the McGuffin that will bring all these characters we've just met together.

We ultimately discover in this presentation of character that the only characters who are remotely similar are Nick (William Hurt) and the dead Alex (Kevin Costner). Since Alex is dead there's no complication in the sense that there is a conflict between similar characters. In a way, Nick replaces Alex (with the former ending up with Chloe), and each member of the ensemble is individualized in relation to the others in the cast who have clearly been established in the first 10 percent of the script. There is also a clear story arc, because the film begins in death and, through Meg, ends in life—it's Meg's most fervent desire to have a child, and through the good graces of Sarah and the good services of Harold, her wish is granted. What appears to be of critical importance in dealing with aspects of character in major and minor ensemble films is to establish clear differences between and among characters, especially when characters are of similar ages and similar experiences. For example, in a minor ensemble film like *Breaking Away* because they are all adolescents with the same limited experiences, you have to establish differences in their attitudes and interests (e.g., Dave's cycling, Mike's rebelliousness). In *The Big Chill*, though the characters are approximately the same age, their individual experiences since graduating from college would have been significantly different and one can draw upon those various experiences to help round out character.

In all of these examples, there are several things in operation that are within the purview of the screenwriter:

1. how each character is conceived (i.e., individualized)
2. how each character is situated in his or her milieu
3. how the elements of the physical, dictional, motivational, historical, relational, and psychological are all presented

In the formation of character, we see how the character is individualized; we see what makes a particular character unique and how that character differs from the other characters in the cast. We also see the role that difference plays, not only in how the character acts, that is, his or her behavior, but, and most dramatically, in what the character says and how he or she says it.

A character's dialogue will carry a great deal of the weight of that character's being and transformation, both of which are vital in any arc an individual character makes in his or her journey, which leads me to the next chapter, on quests.

EXERCISE

Create your own character dossier. In other words, once you've created a character, try to individualize that character in ways that will make that character memorable. What ways can you do that? Have you established the items of the physical, vocal, motivational, historical, relational, and psychological?

WORKS CITED

Forster, E. M. 1955. *Aspects of the Novel*. San Diego: Harcourt Brace Jovanovich.

Kasdan, Lawrence, and Barbara Benedek. 1982. *The Big Chill*.

Sargent, Alvin. 1979. *Ordinary People*.

Stallone, Sylvester. 1976. *Rocky*. Ring Productions.

Tesich, Steve. 1978. *Breaking Away*.

4

SCENE

The Quest, or Where Is
This Hero Going?

IN 1988, I WAS INVITED TO SPEAK AT A CONFERENCE IN ST. PAUL, Minnesota, sponsored by the Romance Writer's Association of America. It was a curious invitation because I never had anything to do with romance writing, but they invited me and several other people to talk about different aspects of film and film writing. Among those invited was Chris Vogler, whom you may know as the author of *The Writer's Journey* (1992). What intrigued me about what Chris talked about was how he used Joseph Campbell's work *The Hero with a Thousand Faces* (1949) since I was using Campbell's work at the same time. The substance of what Vogler was talking about became the basis for his book, which presents a rather unique view of the writing process, using Campbell as a point of departure. What I'd like to do in this chapter is take up Campbell's work in detail to see how you can utilize it in terms of creating a cinematic structure for your story.

The aspects of protagonist, antagonist, predicament, objective, and crisis that I've been talking about fit into a rather unique pattern that comes from Campbell's *The Hero with a Thousand Faces*. Campbell's text draws extensively from world mythologies and on the works of psychology to approach the quest of the hero as an exercise in personal enlightenment and self-fulfillment. It is actually a spiritual journey of the self through the acts of self-discovery but works as a unique approach to story structure as well.

Campbell writes, "The standard path of the mythological adventure of the hero is a magnification of the formula represented in the rites of passage: separation, initiation, return. . . . A hero ventures forth from the world of common day into a region of supernatural wonder: fabulous forces are there encountered and a decisive victory is won: the hero comes back from this mysterious adventure with the power to bestow boons on his fellow man" (1949, 30). This journey transcends both time and culture. Whether the hero is from west or east, north or south, "the adventure of the hero normally follows the pattern of the nuclear unit above described: a separation from the world, a penetration to some source of power, and a life-enhancing return" (35). Examples of this sort abound: Jesus, Buddha, Moses, Prometheus; any hero will invariably go through these stages. "Typically the hero of the fairy tale achieves a domestic microcosmic triumph, and the hero of a myth a world-historical macrocosmic triumph" (37–38). In other words, in the myth, the hero returns with something that will revitalize the immediate or extended community as a whole, but he also returns with something for himself. What the hero returns with may not necessarily be something tangible but may, in fact, be something intangible such as courage or self-esteem or love, but in the end the hero must return with something to make the quest worthwhile.

The macrocosmic scheme of this quest is simplified in three stages:

- departure or separation
- initiation
- return

Within each of these major sections come subsections, seventeen to be exact, not all of them utilized in cinematic plots of the hero because in the majority of cases those subsections concern themselves with notions of spirituality that don't exactly fit within a cinematic story frame-work. But the usefulness of Campbell's work in terms of story structure unifies the act of storytelling and, to a great extent, offers a kind of script blueprint for one to follow. Filmmakers like George Lucas acknowledge their debt to Campbell, while his influence can clearly be seen in the films directed by Spielberg and Zemeckis as well as ex–Monty Pythoners Terry Jones and Terry Gilliam, among others. So let's adapt Campbell's text and focus on its storytelling aspects.

In many commercial films—and all uniquely quest films such as *The Name of the Rose*, *Indiana Jones*, *Romancing the Stone*, *The Matrix*, and *The Fisher King*—the hero will inevitably experience a number of obstacles, which are integrated into the three acts of an Aristotelian play. These three Aristotelian acts are complemented by the three phases Campbell alludes to in the rite of passage:

ACT I
The Aristotelian setup is the equivalent of Campbell's separation.

ACT II
The Aristotelian development is the equivalent of Campbell's initiation.

ACT III
The Aristotelian resolution is the equivalent of Campbell's return.

Let's begin with a comparison of Aristotelian and Campbellian functions of the plot in relation to the plot of *Rocky*.

ACT I
THE PLOT SETUP/THE HERO'S
DEPARTURE OR SEPARATION

1. introduces the main character(s) within a particular venue (Rocky, Adrian, South Philadelphia)
2. establishes a framework for a problem or conflict (Rocky's and Adrian's lack of self-esteem)
3. Presents the objective of the main character (to overcome the image of being a bum)
4. presents incidents that will propel the story forward (Apollo's decision to choose Rocky as an opponent)
5. the hero commits him- or herself to endure the hardships that accompany attainment of the objective(s) (Rocky accepts the challenge)

ACT II
THE PLOT DEVELOPMENT/THE HERO'S INITIATION

1. presents obstacles, conflicts, and subplots to the hero's attempts at attaining the objective(s) (Rocky's conflicts with Paulie and Mickey; Apollo's derision; Adrian's conflict with Paulie; Rocky's lack of conditioning, etc.)

2. moves the dramatic potential forward to its inevitable conclusion (Rocky's training; Adrian's transformation)

ACT III
THE PLOT RESOLUTION/THE HERO'S RETURN

1. the struggle between good and evil (Rocky battles Apollo)
2. the objective is met (Rocky goes the distance; bum motif resolved)
3. happy ending (Rocky and Adrian express their love for each other)

Now let's take this one step further into the specifics of Campbell's quest:

ACT I
THE SETUP/DEPARTURE/SEPARATION

1. call to adventure
2. refusal of the call or the reluctant hero
3. supernatural aid or introduction of the mentor
4. crossing of the first threshold
5. the belly of the whale

ACT II
THE DEVELOPMENT/INITIATION

6. the road of trials
7. the meeting with the goddess
8. woman as the temptress
9. atonement with the father
10. apotheosis
11. the ultimate boon

ACT III
THE RESOLUTION/RETURN

12. refusal of the return
13. the magic flight
14. rescue from without
15. the crossing of the return threshold
16. master of the two worlds
17. freedom to live

Though much of Campbell's work sounds complicated, it really isn't. I'd like to simplify it and go through each of the stages he presents to see how it can be utilized to fit into a structural scheme that will help you in the organization of your story line. Let's begin with the call to adventure.

THE STAGES OF THE HERO'S JOURNEY
The Call to Adventure

This stage is the beginning of the hero's journey and often, but not always, begins with what Campbell recognizes as a blunder or something that implies the merest chance that reveals to the hero an unsuspected world, and the hero is drawn into a relationship with forces that are not entirely understood (Campbell 1949, 51). It may not be a blunder at all, but "some passing phenomenon [that] catches the wandering eye and lures one away from the frequented paths of man" (58). In either case, the blunder or phenomenon "may amount to the opening of a destiny" (51) and in that notion of destiny lay the true beginning of the tale.

Recall, for example, the blunder in the opening of the film *Brazil* as a fly, accidentally crushed in a futuristic typewriter, changes the spelling of a name, alters the direction of the story and creates a quest for Jonathon Pryce's character; or recall in Diane Thomas' *Romancing the Stone* the sudden appearance of a mysterious package that will eventually send Kathleen Turner's character on an adventure/quest to Colombia. According to Campbell, "the call rings up the curtain, always, on a mystery of transfiguration, a rite, or moment, of spiritual passage, which, when complete, amounts to a dying and a birth" (51). The dying and birth are, of course, metaphorical, and the spiritual passage is often substituted with a modification in attitude in the protagonist, which is what I've discussed as the character's arc. It is the transformation the protagonist eventually undergoes affected by events established throughout the course of the film but primarily in the first two acts.

To Campbell, this call to adventure "signifies that destiny has summoned the hero and transferred his spiritual center of gravity from within the pale of his society to a zone unknown" (58). In other words, the accident will take the character from a known place to an unknown one. As Campbell suggests, the new place can be both a region of treasure and a region of danger and can take the appearance of a distant land (e.g., Colombia in *Romancing the Stone*); a forest (*Labyrinth, Robin Hood*); a secret island (*Dr. Moreau*); an underground kingdom (*Indiana Jones and the Temple of Doom*); a new world (*The Matrix, The Wizard of Oz*); or even a panoply of seemingly foreign places within a known place (e.g., *Thelma and Louise, The Fugitive, North by Northwest*), in which the characters are still within a relatively known environment though they have become foreign to it.

Wherever it may be, it is a place not frequented before. Even films as seemingly disparate as the 1995 Academy Award winner for Best Foreign Language Film, *Antonia's Line*, and Disney's *Toy Story* have these things in common: the former returns the main character to her home after World War II, thus, in an ironic way, casting the village of her home as both a recognizable and a foreign place; in the latter, both Buzz and Woody, who begin as antagonists, are separated from the friendly confines of Andy's bedroom in the old house, are initiated to the delinquent Sid's bedroom, then escape and return to Andy's bedroom in the new house as the best of friends.

If one is going to move a character from a venue of comfortability to one of anxiety, one first has to establish the character in that ordinary environment. The reason for establishing that old environment is to create a contrast with the new environment. As I said, the venue may involve a physical shift *from* a place like home *to* a place totally unlike home (as in *The Matrix*); or it may be an emotional or psychological shift *within* home (as in *Breaking Away*); or it can be like the main character, Renton, in *Trainspotting*, who must move from an environment of "heroin dependence" to an environment of "heroin independence."

In *Ordinary People*, Conrad's move is from the uncomfortably comfortable world of his home and daily life to the uncomfortably uncomfortable world of Berger, the psychiatrist, who forces him to confront the psychological obstacles that keep him from overcoming the guilt he has for his brother's death. In *Il Postino*, the mailman goes from the routine and comfortable world of delivering mail to the uncomfortable world of falling in love and seeking guidance from none other than Nobel Laureate Pablo Neruda. In *Thelma and Louise*, for example, we see both women leaving the confines of their rather boring daily lives to enter a completely different world the moment that Louise murders the would-be rapist. They move from the daily confines of conventionality to the anxious expanse of becoming fugitives.

In *The Fisher King*, Jack Lucas goes from being a wealthy and arrogant radio jock to a humble and reclusive video clerk who finds redemption through the figure of Parry. Rocky goes from being a bum boxer in South Philadelphia to becoming a champion heavyweight contender. In *The Graduate*, Benjamin goes from being an indecisive college undergraduate to becoming a graduate with adult problems; in *Midnight Cowboy*, Joe Buck goes from country stud to urban caretaker; in *Elizabeth*, the heroine goes from being the bastard child of King Henry to becoming the Queen of England; in *Life Is Beautiful*, Guido makes the ultimate change from being a free man to an imprisoned and then executed man. The examples are as endless as the films. But we can see that implied in this call to adventure is the presentation of a problem, a challenge, or an objective that must be satisfied by the end of the film, because the hero can no longer remain untouched by living in the tranquility of the everyday world. As Campbell says, "The familiar life horizon has been outgrown; the old concepts, ideals, and emotional patterns no longer fit; the time for the passing of a threshold is at hand" (51). To remain home would mean no conflict, and no conflict means no story.

Regardless of the type of plot—action adventure, mystery, romantic comedy—the call to adventure initiates the action of the story. Without it, there is no story line. Whatever the case may be, it involves a change of direction, a change of purpose, and implicit in any change is the potential of conflict. However, one may not want to deal with conflict because conflict is uncomfortable. So what we often end up with is a refusal of the call.

Refusal of the Call

"Often in actual life," Campbell writes, "and not infrequently in the myths and popular tales, we encounter the dull case of the call unanswered; for it is always possible to turn the ear to other interests. Refusal of the summons converts the adventure into its negative. . . . The myths and folk tales of the whole world make clear that the refusal is essentially a refusal to give up what one takes to be one's own interest" (59–60).

In other words, at this point, the hero may resist. After all, the hero doesn't know what's going to happen out there beyond the safety of the known environment. In mythology and folktales the story often goes no farther than this; but if that were the case in screenplays, our scripts would be short indeed. There may be a hesitation on the hero's part—a momentary restitution of the place that is most comfortable—but for the story to be told in earnest, refusal of the call to adventure is unacceptable.

At this stage, we discover that there is something that prohibits the hero from making the move, of initiating the change, of attempting the break from the comfortability of the common world. In *Rocky*, after Rocky's been selected by Apollo Creed and informed by Jurgens that he is not to be a mere "sparring partner," but an "opponent," he has doubts about whether he should fight or not; after all, everyone thinks he's a bum, and he has reservations himself. In *Ordinary People*, Conrad isn't sure he wants to make an appointment with a psychiatrist because that's going to get him in touch with his feelings about the death of his brother, something he longs to repress. In *The Graduate*, Benjamin is totally against any involvement with Mrs. Robinson, especially after she confronts him in the nude. In *Braveheart*, William Wallace is content to live peacefully on his land until he realizes he can't have the woman he loves unless he takes a Scottish position against the British and murders some Brits.

But something does drive these characters to seek higher ground. There is something that motivates the hero to take action, to seize the opportunity. According to Campbell, there is a "rejection of the offered terms of life, as a result of which some power of transformation carries the problem to a plane of new magnitudes, where it is suddenly and finally resolved" (65). In other words, when the hero rejects the everyday life and embarks on something new, two things present themselves:

1. the implied acceptance that potential problems (conflicts/obstacles) may arise
2. the implied recognition that the new journey will be resolved in some fashion

So, whatever the case may be, we see some variation of the resistant hero; but when we have a hero who's somewhat resistant about taking the next step, what's the best way to help the hero change his or her mind? Perhaps the hero needs some kind of help, some kind of guidance—some supernatural aid or a mentor.

Supernatural Aid, or the Mentor

"For those who have not refused the call," Campbell writes, "the first encounter of the hero-journey is with a protective figure (often a little old crone or old man) who provides the adventurer with amulets against the dragon forces he is about to pass" (69). This particular figure represents the "benign, protecting power of destiny" (71). "The higher mythologies develop the role in the great figure of the guide, the teacher, the ferryman, the conductor of souls to the afterworld" (72). So where does this figure enter in film scripts?

Well, we often find someone who will teach and/or assist the hero in accomplishing something. Now this something may not appear to be positive at the outset, but it may have positive value. For example, unlikely as it may seem, in Buck Henry's script *The Graduate*, Mrs. Robinson is really Benjamin's mentor. He learns a great deal from her: she incites him to anger, causes him to confront authority, and challenges him to be responsible for his actions, even though these things are not explicitly stated.

In Waldo Salt's brilliant script *Midnight Cowboy*, Ratso Rizzo becomes Joe Buck's urban tutor, though a kind of mutual mentoring goes on throughout the story, with John Voight's character finally taking care of Ratso in the end. In *Rocky*, Mickey, the wizened old boxing coach, comes to share his wealth of boxing knowledge and experience with Rocky, even though Rocky at first denies him the opportunity. In *Ordinary People*, the psychiatrist, Berger, helps Conrad get through the psychological turmoil from which he's suffering. In *Good Will Hunting*, Robin Williams reprises Judd Hirsch's role in *Ordinary People*. In *Il Postino* Pablo Neruda helps the pathetic postman capture his love through the majesty of metaphors. In *The Cook, the Thief, His Wife and Her Lover*, a case could certainly be made for Michael, the lover, as being Georgina's mentor. In *Braveheart*, Wallace's uncle becomes his guardian shortly after the murder of Wallace's father, and even though we see him only in passing, his teachings manifest themselves in the way Wallace behaves as an adult and a leader. Certainly in *The Matrix* Laurence Fishburne's character mentors Keanu Reeves' character. The mentor may also appear as the polished scholar or sophisticated male (*Educating Rita*, *My Fair Lady*) or the master martial artist (*Karate Kid*) or the observant monk (*The Name of the Rose*) or a damsel's dashing savior (*Romancing the Stone*). The list goes on forever.

Whatever the case may be, the mentor's primary function is to assist the hero in addressing the anxieties of the unknown and assisting the hero in the transformation. However, the mentor can assume more than one role. For example, though one can say that Michael is Georgina's mentor, that Michael Douglas is Kathleen Turner's guide, that Mrs. Robinson is Benjamin's teacher, they are also love/sex interests. The two are not mutually exclusive, it merely depends on how one chooses to use the mentor.

By the same token, the role of the mentor is limited. As Vogler writes, "Eventually the hero must face the unknown alone" (1992, 22). Rocky climbs into the ring with Apollo; Conrad must come to terms with the person who needs the most forgiveness; Benjamin needs to go beyond being the graduate. So the mentor assists the hero in his or her journey and with that comes a movement from one space to another that demands that the hero cross the first threshold.

Crossing of the First Threshold

"With the personification of his destiny to guide and aid him," Campbell writes, "the hero goes forward in his adventure until he comes to the 'threshold guardian' at the entrance to the zone of magnified power. . . . Beyond them are darkness, the unknown and danger. . . . The usual person is more than content, he is even proud, to remain within the indicated bounds, and popular belief gives him every reason to fear so much as the first step into the unexplored" (1949, 77–78). We already know that the hero cannot stay within the boundaries of the normal, everyday world. In other words, she or he can't stay "home alone." The hero must commit to the quest, and by committing to the quest, crosses the first threshold into a new world. Rocky accepts Apollo's challenge; Benjamin calls Mrs. Robinson; Conrad visits the psychiatrist; Joe Buck leaves Texas; Wallace slits an Englishman's throat. At that point, the hero agrees—at least in principle, if not in fact—to confront the consequences of such a decision.

As I've discussed, for Aristotle, the most important thing is the structuring of the incidents and the Aristotelian acts can be regarded as representing a beginning, a middle, and an end. It is at this point that the hero makes a decision that will become unchangeable and that will lead him or her to the inevitable conclusion established at the outset. In other words, the decision made at this point will eventually unify the ending with the beginning, or as Aristotle has said, link the beginning to the end with inevitable certainty. This decision to move forward clearly ends one way of the hero's being and creates a new way of being because the inevitable outcome of the decision to act will invariably affect the hero's constitution. So, in effect, this crossing of the first threshold is also the crossing from the beginning to the middle or from Act I to Act II, or from the setup of incidents to the development of the incidents. But Campbell suggests there is still one more stage to go through before the hero can justifiably become initiated, and that is entering the belly of the whale.

The Belly of the Whale

In cinematic stories, this stage is really an extension of stage 4 because this stage gives renewed emphasis "to the lesson that the passage of the threshold is a form of self-annihilation" (91). In other words, it means that, by accepting the challenge presented to him or her, the hero has agreed to "kill" whoever he or she was prior to the acceptance of the call and has agreed to accept what might happen. In a way, it's like being born again.

Essentially, the crossing of the first threshold concludes the first act. In other words, stages 1 through 4 plus 5 constitute the first act of the play. Campbell's first five segments are equivalent to Aristotle's Act I, which sets up what's going to happen through the course of the story and to whom it's going to happen.

In effect, crossing the first threshold is tantamount to the transition between Acts I and II, in which the hero, who has now accepted the challenge, moves from the comfortable and mundane world into the foreign world of obstacles. Perhaps anxious, but no longer reluctant, the hero must now learn whatever there is to learn about the world outside him- or herself and, consequently, about him- or herself. Essentially, this is the boundary—real or imaginary—the protagonist crosses, and this is the cinematic moment at which point the story will take a different direction.

This is the moment when Rocky says yes to Apollo; when Benjamin calls Mrs. Robinson; when Conrad visits the psychiatrist; when Kathleen Turner embarks for Colombia; when Renton, in *Trainspotting*, decides to kick the heroin habit. In short, it is the moment when the hero chooses to seek his or her destiny.

This segment concludes the separation phase. But in one's quest to become a hero, to be initiated as a hero, a number of obstacles will present themselves, which as a collection constitute the road of trials.

The Road of Trials

"Once having traversed the threshold," Campbell writes, "the hero moves in a dream landscape of curiously fluid, ambiguous forms, where he must survive a succession of trials. [This phase] has produced a world literature of miraculous tests and ordeals" (97). Though the mentor has assisted the hero, the hero must continue the journey primarily on his or her own. Now the hero will encounter all sorts of challenges, "physical, psychological, emotional," that will test the fabric of his or her being.

It may be a psychological grappling that one must deal with, as in *Ordinary People*; or, in *Rocky*, it may be the constant doubts he has not only about his ability as a boxer but as a human being; or, in *The Graduate*, it may be the sanctions imposed on Benjamin by Mrs. Robinson, as well as Elaine's hostility toward him for allegedly raping her mother; or it may be Charles Smithson's repressed desires for Sarah in Harold Pinter's script of *The French Lieutenant's Woman*.

These trials may present physical obstacles as well. For example, "The hero may come to a dangerous place, sometimes deep underground, where the object of the quest is hidden" (Vogler 1992, 24). It may be the antagonist's hideaway. When the hero enters that space, he or she is now within the phase of the initiation. *Indiana Jones and the Temple of Doom* reveals the horrible venue of that film, as does *Jurassic Park*. In practically any James Bond film, it's the headquarters of the villain (e.g., *Dr. No*,

Goldfinger, Never Say Never Again), but it may appear in other forms as well depending on the nature of the story.

We can see how the hero functions under physical, psychological, or emotional stress and how that stress will have a bearing on the character's arc. As Campbell writes, "The original departure into the land of trials represented only the beginning of the long and really perilous path of initiatory conquests and moments of illumination. Dragons have now to be slain and surprising barriers passed—again, again, and again" (1949, 108). In other words, it is not one trial that the hero has to overcome, but a multitude of trials, a road of trials. As we've seen in *Rain Man*, Charlie Babbitt must not only get over his own egotistic and selfish nature but be able to learn continually how to care for and recognize the limitations of his autistic brother. It is only then that the hero can meet the goddess.

The Meeting with the Goddess

"The ultimate adventure," says Campbell, "when all the barriers and ogres have been overcome, is commonly represented as a mystical marriage of the triumphant hero-soul with the Queen Goddess of the World" (109). This is a particularly problematic phase to deal with in cinematic stories, and Campbell writes that "through this exercise [the hero's] spirit is purged of its infantile, inappropriate sentimentalities and resentments, and his mind [is] opened to the inscrutable presence which exits, not primarily as 'good' and 'bad' with respect to his childlike human convenience . . . but as the law and image of the nature of being" (114). In simple terms, the protagonist grows up, and Campbell suggests that woman represents the totality of what can be known in this growing-up process because "she is the guide to the sublime acme of sensuous adventure" (116).

One might be able to synthesize this particular phase as "boy gets girl," but only because the girl has allowed him. He becomes the king of her created world. We see this relationship most often in romantic comedies in which the seed for the union between two people is planted very early. This relationship, which may not be functionally active at the outset of the story (e.g., as Mrs. Robinson seduces Benjamin she also introduces both he and the audience to her daughter, Elaine—the eventual love interest—via her portrait), has been established within the first percent of the film. In *Four Weddings and a Funeral*, Andie MacDowell is the goddess, and the bungling Hugh Grant is the hero, who, after surviving a panoply of trials, finally gets what he wanted all along. We also see this in other films such as *Crocodile Dundee*, *Indiana Jones*, *Sleepless in Seattle*, *Romancing the Stone*, *You've Got Mail*, *Clones*, *Green Card*, and any one of a number of romantic and/or adventure comedies (often starring Andie MacDowell) in which the romantic setup in the first act and developed in the second act pays off in the third act. Not coincidentally, it is after Charlie has the revelations about who Raymond really is that he calls Susan, who forgives him and subsequently meets him in Las Vegas. "The meeting with the goddess—who is present in every woman—is the final test of the talent of the hero to win the boon of love, which is life itself enjoyed as the casement of eternity" (118). After going through all the trials and tribulations presented to our hero, he then achieves the love he has been pursuing. This particular phase is linked with the woman as temptress.

Woman as the Temptress

This phase is also a bit problematic in terms of defining what is going on with the hero, but in this case, the hero must "surpass the temptations of her call, and soar to the immaculate ether beyond" (122). Obviously there is the temptation of the flesh involved and "woman above all, become[s] the symbol no longer of victory but of defeat" (123). Certainly women like this are not new in film; the *femme fatale* is not a new idea. In any James Bond film the temptress is ever-present and is usually juxtaposed with the goddess, who eventually wins out; but one can also see it in a film like *Fatal Attraction* or any of a number of *Fatal Attraction* clones. We can obviously expand this notion of the woman being a source of defeat to now include the homme fatale. In either case, there appears to be one person set against another, and the genuine love of one tends to offset the evil intents of the other, resulting in some kind of victory for the hero. One could look at the relationship between Elaine and Mrs. Robinson in this context.

The stage is included within the initiation phase because it may be yet one more obstacle the hero must overcome in order to secure hero-hood. But there may still be others, such as atonement with the father.

Atonement with the Father

This particular stage deals primarily with the psychological manifestations demonstrated in father-son issues, though, by extension, one can use father surrogates if fathers are not present.

Just as one example, in *Rocky*, Rocky alludes to the fact that his father may be dead. That is, when he talks about his father, it's always in the past tense. There is no father figure for Rocky, so Mickey becomes both a mentor and a father surrogate, and in the confrontational meeting between the two of them, both Rocky and Mickey make amends after Mickey humbles himself in Rocky's presence. This phase involves some "hope and assurance from the helpful female figure, by whose magic the hero is protected through all the frightening experiences of the father's ego-shattering initiation" (Campbell 1949, 131). Certainly, Rocky's relationship with Adrian may have, in some way, modified Rocky's character, and one can see how, in a character-driven script in which there is a triangular situation among the hero and female/male supporting character and a father, this situation may manifest. Certainly in a film like *Ordinary People*, Conrad's love interest has had an impact on how he deals not only with his friends but also with his father and mother. But it would appear that this particular phase is dependent on the dramatic potential of the story line and that story line would have to include some aspect of father-son conflict for it to have any value in the script.

Apotheosis, or Deification

This stage can also be a bit problematic to utilize as a marker in structuring a feature screenplay, because the stage itself entails the reaching of a divine state of being for the hero, who has gone beyond the last terrors of ignorance. For Campbell, it represents "the release potential within us all and which anyone can attain—through hero hood" (151). This phase has been somewhat altered to present the apotheosis, or deification, of the supreme ordeal. Essentially, this is the revelation stage of the initiation phase. "The ogre breaks us, but the hero, the fit candidate, undergoes the initiation 'like a man' " (161). Here is the confrontation between the "life-wish" (Eros) and the "death-wish" (Thanatos) that "are the two drives that not only move the individual from within but also animate for him the surrounding world" (164). In other words, the hero must escape his own ego and attain something higher in order to continue the quest to its just completion.

This stage is not so easily created in film structure, since it is precisely the androgynous integration of the male and the female, the two into the one, which doesn't really translate well to film and especially Hollywood film. We can alter the stage to the point at which one can determine it to be a true moment of revelation (after Aristotle) at which time the hero recognizes something larger than him- or herself needs to be accomplished and then incorporates that into him- or herself in order to make him- or herself total.

So, for Benjamin, the revelation, which really becomes a quest is: Has what he has learned about himself and Elaine been enough for him to save her from a marriage that won't work? For Rocky: Has what he has learned about himself been enough for him to fight Apollo? For Conrad: Has what he has learned about himself given him the courage to confront issues about his dead brother? For the postman: Has what he has learned about himself enabled him to express his love for the most beautiful girl in the village? For Bill Murray in *Groundhog Day*: Has what he has learned about himself finally enabled him to get it right? In short, it is a moment of deification, in the simplest sense, in that the hero acknowledges that she or he is something that she or he was not before. By reaching such a stage, then, the hero should be rewarded with something—the ultimate boon.

The Ultimate Boon

As Campbell writes, "the boon is simply a symbol of life energy stepped down to the requirements of a certain specific case" (188). The boon can be a request made with authority or the thing requested. As a thing requested, it can take the shape of something that will enable the hero to see better. In effect, it becomes a kind of trophy for experiencing and overcoming the road of trials.

In *Breaking Away*, Dave tapes his injured feet to the pedals, rides to victory, and claims the Little 500 bike trophy as recompense for his trials. In *The Graduate*, Benjamin literally seizes a cross, locks Elaine's family and friends inside the church, and claims her as his trophy. "Going the distance" becomes Rocky's trophy. In *Indiana Jones*, he retrieves the sacred stone, which becomes the trophy. In *Romancing the Stone*, the emerald becomes the trophy. *Trophy* is the appropriate word because a trophy is anything that serves as a token or evidence of victory, valor, power, skill, and so on. But the trophy may merely be the symbolic representation of what the hero has finally discovered about him- or herself. In *Rain Man*, Charlie Babbitt's trophy is, quite simply, the understanding of what love means. In *The Matrix*, it is Keanu Reeves' recognition that he actually is the chosen one. Ideally, the hero should have learned something from the experience, which makes the person a better-rounded human being. In that sense, it completes the character arc that was established at the outset.

All of these things—both tangible and intangible—can be considered trophies, and the attainment of such generally concludes the initiation phase and leads to the last phase: the return.

Refusal of the Return

As Campbell writes, the return trip "requires that the hero shall now begin the labor of bringing the runes of wisdom, the Golden Fleece, or his sleeping princess back into the kingdom of humanity, where the boon may redound to the renewing of the community" (193). This stage initiates the return phase. In myth, the responsibility is sometimes refused, but in film that would put a damper on the climax, so there can be no refusal of the return. But, there may be a magic flight.

The Magic Flight

What usually happens in this phase is that the "trophy has been attained against the opposition of its guardian, or if the hero's wish to return to the world has been resented by the gods or demons, then the last stage . . . [often] becomes a lively, often comical, pursuit . . . complicated by marvels of magical obstruction and evasion" (197). This stage is what can also be called the retreat from danger or the flight from fear. For example, though Indiana Jones retrieves the stone for the people of India, he still has to return the stone to its proper guardians and is pursued on the way back. Bond, who always seems to come up with the girl at the end of the film, is always chased by the evil wrongdoers whom he thinks he's already finished off. It's the kind of backfire element that one finds regardless of the type of script being written. Essentially, it is that point in the film in which the hero has accomplished all that she or he thinks needs to be accomplished; yet there remains one outstanding obstacle to overcome. In such cases it is imperative that the hero receive rescue from without.

Rescue from Without

"The hero may have to be brought back from his supernatural adventure by assistance from without," says Campbell. "That is to say, the world may have to come and get him" (207). As I indicated, this situation always seems to happen to Bond, in which he's gotten himself in too deeply and needs to be bailed out. But this situation is not necessarily Bond-dependent. It usually happens in films in which the army comes to the rescue after the hero has attained the trophy. For example, we see it in such adventures as Last of the Mohicans and Dances with Wolves and in Romancing the Stone when, at the bleakest moment possible, Kathleen Turner is rescued by Michael Douglas. Essentially, it is that moment when the protagonist, at a moment of crisis, is assisted from outside by a compatriot, a rescuer, or a significant other.

This phase, then, brings us to the final crisis, which is the crossing from the mystic realm back into the life of the everyday. "Whether rescued from without, driven from within, or gently carried along by the guiding divinities, he has yet to re-enter with his boon . . . his life-redeeming elixir" (216). So it is here that we finally come to the crossing of the return threshold.

The Crossing of the Return Threshold

"The two worlds, the divine and the human, can be pictured only as distinct from each other—different as life and death, as day and night," writes Campbell. "The hero adventures out of the land we know into darkness; there he accomplishes his adventure . . . and his return is described as a coming back out of that . . . zone" (217). The questions that remain for the hero at this stage are: Why return at all? What could possibly compete with all the trials and tribulations of initiation that the hero has gone through? But "the returning hero, to complete his adventure, must survive the impact of the world" (226).

This is the equivalent of reentry. Rocky, beaten and bloody, goes the distance, and is being resurrected, as the beginning suggests, as a heavyweight contender, not as a bum. Benjamin goes against all the odds—both mathematical and moral—and captures Elaine, who's already attired for marriage. Baskerville, in The Name of the Rose, survives the flames of hell, which happen to be in a monastery, and escapes the labyrinth with as many manuscripts as he can carry; Charlie Babbitt finally loves; and Conrad finally cries.

Unless a trophy is brought back from the initiation, the hero has not been justly initiated and therefore has learned nothing; if the hero has learned nothing, then there's no story unless, of course, the learning of nothing, which is something, is what the hero has learned.

It would seem that this particular stage would conclude the quest of the hero. And to a great extent it does, since the story line has been concluded, the arc of the hero has been finished, and the problems have been resolved. But Campbell speaks of two more stages.

Master of the Two Worlds
Freedom to Live

These last two stages are generally disregarded in terms of structuring a standard feature screenplay. Master of the two worlds is that stage in which the hero has somehow been transfigured. By suffering the road of trials, he has mastered the world he came from and, presumably, will now be better suited to master the world to which he has returned. "Presumably, the 'freedom to live' allows the hero to be the champion of things [that are] becoming, not of things [that have been], since he now *is*" (Campbell 1949, 243).

In a curious way, though, these two stages could be looked upon as preparatory stages for a sequel or sequels, in that the hero has learned something important, and that learning will, in some way, prepare him for other stages in his life. One could make an argument that these two stages are a kind of preconditioning exercise for subsequent films since the ending of the first film lays the foundation for the second; the second, the third; and so on. We could follow Rocky, for example, throughout the sequels to see if, in fact, this would work, but, as in the Bond films, there remains the "virtue of the repetitively constant" to enable the story to succeed, and to that extent, each script merely repeats, with modifications, the situation established in the original story and carries that character forward.

In conclusion, Campbell's quest of the hero can be schematized in the following way:

1. The hero sets forth from his everyday life (ordinary world).

2. Someone or something suddenly transfers the hero to the threshold of adventure (call to adventure).

3. The hero balks at the unknown (reluctance).

4. There he encounters a presence that assists him (mentor).

5. He then has to overcome a road of trials (obstacles).

6. When he arrives at the bottom, he overcomes a supreme obstacle and gains his reward (trophy).

7. The triumph may be represented as the hero's sexual union with the goddess-mother (marriage), his recognition by the father-creator (atonement), his own divination (apotheosis), or, if the powers have been unfriendly, his theft of the boon he came to gain.

8. The final work is that of the return. If the powers have blessed the hero, he now sets forth under their protection.

9. At the return threshold the powers must remain behind; the hero reemerges from the kingdom of dread (return, resurrection).

10. The boon that he brings restores both him and the world. (Campbell 1949, 245–46)

We can compare this scheme with the script framework:

It begins with compelling hook that establishes who the main character(s) is and what she or he does.

- The setting and time period of the story have been established.
- It tells whose story it is (i.e., it introduces the central and supporting characters).
- Conflicts have been established that initiate and propel the story line.
- All of these lead to a climax.
- The climax results in a well-defined resolution.

And that scheme is what constitutes the hero myth of the movies in combination with the Aristotelian dramatic framework. The two of them work in unison, but Campbell's scheme is not a template merely to put over your story and match up completely; rather, it can assist you in structuring the spine of your script and it should be used accordingly. It is, of course, only one approach to scripting a plot line. There are others, and I'll look at another one in the next chapter.

EXERCISE

Create a chart with three columns. In the first column, write down the Campbellian scheme; in the second, the Aristotelian scheme. Then choose a film of your liking and pick out where these schemes coincide with the film you're watching. Note those markers. Are they similar? Do they work within the framework of the film itself? Then apply them to your own script to see how well they work or don't work.

WORKS CITED

Campbell, Joseph. 1949. *The Hero with a Thousand Faces*. New York: Pantheon Books.

Vogler, Chris. 1992. *The Writer's Journey: Mythic Structures for Screenwriters and Storytellers*. Studio City, CA: M. Wiese Productions.

5

SCENE

Plots, or Where Else Is This Hero Going?

I'VE SPENT CONSIDERABLE TIME TALKING ABOUT CAMPBELL AND Aristotle and how their individual approaches can be utilized in relation to structuring a standard feature screenplay. Now I'd like to introduce another approach to help broaden your options. Northrop Frye's *Anatomy of Criticism* (1957) is a text devoted mainly to the study of literary texts, but it can be of help in categorizing different types of plots and in using those categories to develop a structure for your screenplay.

In his essay on archetypes titled "Theory of Mythos," Frye divides literary narratives into five major categories, which can also be utilized in screenplay structure. These five main types of mythical movements are:

- the comic/romantic
- the romantic/adventure
- the romantic/quest
- the tragic
- the satiric

Now I will consider all five individually and discuss how they relate to standard screenplay structure.

THE COMIC/ROMANTIC

Though when Frye talks about comedy, he's talking about particular literary texts, we can extend that approach to include romantic comedies or dramatic comedies such as *When Harry Met Sally*, *The Heartbreak Kid*, *Sleepless in Seattle, You've Got Mail,* or *Four Weddings and a Funeral* because what Frye has to say about comedy in relation to literary texts is certainly applicable to these particular films.

According to Frye, what often happens in this kind of story is that "a young man wants a young woman, that his desire is resisted by some opposition, usually paternal, and that near the end of the play some twist in the plot enables the hero to have his will" (1957, 163). The story line moves from one layer of society to another. In other words, the movement is from a marginalized society to an acceptable, if not bourgeois, society. The obstructing characters at the beginning of the play are generally in charge of the play's society and at the end the hero and heroine create a new society, which is frequently signalized by a party or a ritual (e.g., a wedding) (163).

The obstacles to the hero's desire, then, form the action of the comedy, and overcoming them forms the comic resolution (164). The main obstacle to the hero attaining his desire, if it is not the father, is generally someone like the father and who comes from that society, that is, "a rival with less youth and more money" (165). "The tendency of comedy is to include as many people as possible in its final society: the blocking characters are more often reconciled or converted rather than repudiated" (165). We also see that comedy moves toward a happy ending and the normal response of the audience to a happy ending is "this is how it should be" (167).

Let's take *Four Weddings and a Funeral* as an example to see if these comedic elements that Frye discusses actually work in film. If we adapt Frye's scheme to *Four Weddings,* we get the following:

1. A young man desires a young woman.

2. His desires are obstructed initially by the young man himself, who's always saying or doing things that will somehow get him into trouble and the obstacles to his desire form the action of the comedy.

3. Though it appears to be too late for their love, he tries to express his love anyway.

4. The true blocking character appears (Hamish, Andie MacDowell's husband-to-be), who not only is the substitute father figure but presumably represents the finality of their love.

5. Resigned to the fact that his ideal love is gone, the young man plans to marry another woman; however, there is a sudden twist at the end when he discovers his true love is divorced and he rejects his fiancée at the altar.

6. Now both single, the two lovers can finally get together.

7. The end reveals a cast of single people now almost all incorporated into the final society of a community of marriage, thus contributing to a happy ending.

Now I'll deal with each part individually.

A *young man desires a young woman.*

In Scene 20 of the Richard Curtis script, the first wedding at the country church, Charles (Hugh Grant) is standing outside with Fiona (Kristin Scott Thomas). Charles has already noticed Carrie (Andie MacDowell) no fewer than three times before this scene. Charles sees Carrie talking to someone's grandmother. Charles asks who she is and Fiona answers that her name is Carrie. Charles says she's pretty; Fiona replies "American." Charles says, "Interesting," and Fiona counters with "Slut." Then she tells him Carrie worked for *Vogue*, but that she's out of his league, to which he responds, "Well, that's a relief. Thanks." So we've already been put on notice that Charles has a keen interest in Carrie and that Carrie is available.

His desires are obstructed initially by the young man himself, who's always saying or doing things that will somehow get him into trouble and the obstacles to his desire form the action of the comedy.

There are two excellent scenes demonstrating this posture. Scene 23 at the reception has Charles on a quest to chat up Carrie. When he finally manages to find her alone and begins to talk to her, John appears, creating a rather awkward situation. Charles asks John how that "gorgeous girlfriend" of his is, to which John replies that she is no longer his girlfriend. In safe retreat, Charles replies that he shouldn't take it too hard since "rumor has it she never stopped bonking old Toby de Lisle, just in case you didn't work out." A somewhat stunned John replies, "She is now my wife," which renders Charles a bit speechless. Incapable of extricating himself, Charles merely congratulates John, while Carrie, somewhat embarrassed by the situation, silently slips away.

The next scene takes place at the Boatman, an inn where Carrie and Charles have spent the night together after the reception. He's startled out of sleep at the sound of a closing zipper and awakes to find Carrie dressed and on her way back to America. She asks when he had anticipated announcing their engagement. Charles, of course, is bemused. "Sorry—whose engagement?" Carrie says, "Ours. I assumed since we'd slept together and everything, we'd be getting married. What did you think?" Charles once again is speechless until he sees she's smiling and realizes it's a joke. But it's not really a joke, for the last thing she says before she leaves is, "But I think we both missed a great opportunity here," after which she leaves and Charles resumes the pose in his bed.

These two scenes expand Charles' character as someone who not only often says the wrong thing at the wrong time but is guilty of not saying the right thing at the right time. Charles is clearly someone who is his own worst enemy in terms of dealing with his emotions.

**Though it appears to be too late for their love,
he tries to express his love anyway.**

On a day off, while looking for yet another wedding present, Charles bumps into Carrie, who's looking for just the right wedding gown. They shop together, stop by a cafe, and chat about the number of previous sexual affairs they've had; Carrie admits to having had a goodly number and Charles only nine. Outside the National Film Theatre, they run into David, Charles' deaf brother, and there's a three-way conversation, all of which for Carrie gets comically lost in the sign language. As Carrie leaves, David and Charles enter the theatre.

Moments later, Charles runs out and catches her on the Embankment near Waterloo Bridge. In a brilliant bit of foppery, Charles finally admits his love for Carrie by saying, "in the words of David Cassidy, in fact, while he was still with the Partridge Family, 'I think I love you,' and I just wondered whether by any chance . . ." and he goes on to founder about then, realizing she's taken already, says, "Never mind," and begins to leave. Of course, Carrie is taken by the admission, says to him, "You're lovely," kisses him on the cheek, and walks away.

It's a bittersweet moment in that they both understand that it's all over between them and they did, in fact, miss a great opportunity.

The true blocking character appears (Hamish, Andie MacDowell's husband-to-be), who not is only the substitute father figure but presumably represents the finality of their love.

Scene 74 takes us to the grand hall of a Scottish manor house. Charles is in the back of the room while Carrie and her husband-to-be, Hamish, are on a raised platform. As she talks to the guests, there are cuts from Carrie to Charles who, by the look on his face, is clearly in love and can't believe "he let her go." She concludes by saying, "Oh, and one more thing—someone here told me confidentially that if things with Hamish didn't work out, that he would step in. I just wanted to say, 'Thanks, and I'll keep you posted.' " Hamish, of course, roars his approval, but, in fact, it's a plot device, which comes to fruition.

We've seen how the story has gradually and methodically moved from a society composed of single people to a society composed of married people; in other words, there has been an integration of presumably unfulfilled single people into the mainstream of presumed marital bliss. This is the third wedding of the four—the one after which we see the funeral—and in the course of the wedding celebrations a number of the guests have now paired off and, presumably, will get married themselves. We've also witnessed the obstacles that Charles must overcome during the story and how those obstacles have become the bases for the comedy itself; for example, his inability to be on time; his difficulty in expressing his feelings; his ineptness in communicating with anyone except his deaf brother, which, in fact, lends itself to the comic irony.

Resigned to the fact that his ideal love is gone, the young man plans to marry another woman; however, there is a sudden twist at the end when he discovers his true love is divorced and he rejects his fiancée at the altar.

This is the fourth wedding, Charles' wedding with Henrietta, who's been after him since the beginning of the film. Immediately before he's about to walk down the aisle, Charles sees Carrie, who gives him the news that she's now divorced. This information gives him misgivings about what he's about to do. Realizing he would be making a terrible mistake, Charles decides at the altar and upon the signing advice of his brother not to marry Henrietta, who promptly punches him in the face and knocks him to the chapel floor.

Now both single, the two lovers can finally get together.
Later that afternoon, Carrie shows up at Charles' house. Charles goes out-side to meet her and they talk. In yet another roundabout way, Charles proposes to Carrie and, amid the rain showers, they kiss.

The end reveals a cast of single people now almost all incorporated into the final society of a community of marriage, thus contributing to a happy ending.
The film concludes with an "album" of snapshots, accompanied by the music "Chapel of Love," with Henrietta finally married to the Royal Guard of her dreams; David and Serena married; Scarlett and Chester married; Tom and Dierdre married; Matthew and his new boyfriend together, if not married; leaving only Fiona unmarried to Prince Charles; and, finally, Charles and Carrie married with their infant son.

So we see how neatly Curtis' script fits within the structure of the romantic comedy that Frye suggests. Almost every individual element Frye has talked about presents itself in the structure of the story and though the word "fuck" is mentioned no fewer than twenty times in the dialogue, the script does a successful job of shaping Charles' character.

THE ROMANTIC/ADVENTURE

The second category Frye talks about is romance. "The romance is [the] nearest of all literary forms to the wish-fulfillment dream" (186); the "essential element of plot in romance is adventure, which means that romance is naturally a sequential and processional form . . . At its most naive it is an endless form in which a central character who never devel-ops or ages goes through one adventure after another" (186).

One can see how this scheme neatly coincides with the Campbellian quest I've already talked about because the "complete form of the romance is clearly the successful quest and such a completed form has three main stages: the stage of the perilous journey and the preliminary minor adven-tures; the crucial struggle, usually some kind of battle in which either the hero or his foe, or both, must die; and the exaltation of the hero" (Frye 1957, 187). Frye also suggests that "the enemy may be an ordinary human being" but may also take on "demonic mythical qualities" (187).

A prime example of cinematic romance with an emphasis on adventure is Diane Thomas' *Romancing the Stone*, which has elements of comedy and romance tied into the quest. In summary, we have romance novelist Joan Wilder (Kathleen Turner) living alone in New York and crying over the endings of her own novels. Her editor is concerned that she'll never find the one she'll be truly happy with, though Wilder disagrees. Wilder receives a mysterious package not long before she gets a phone call from her kidnapped sister telling her that she'll be killed if the package isn't delivered. She goes on an adventure, meets Jack Colton (Michael Douglas), and the two of them eventually turn the contents of package to their advantage even though they are pursued by a panoply of villains.

In the June 23, 1983, revision of the script, the hook that Thomas came up with was opening with the ending to one of Wilder's own romantic westerns in which the heroine, Angelina, is saved from Grogan's evil brothers (the former of whom she's knifed to death) by her hero, Jesse, who chases the brothers. In the film version, these scenes have been dramatically reshaped so that Jesse kills the brothers, picks up Angelina, and rides off with her, while Joan, first in a voice-over, then in a medium shot of her at her typewriter, weeps and says, "And I knew then that Jesse would never disappoint me. He was the man I loved, the one man I could trust. And we would spend the rest of our lives together forever. The end." To celebrate the accomplishment, she and her cat, Romeo, dine alone together.

What we see in the first several minutes is tantamount to the preliminary adventures, which are tied into the opening hook; that is, the "fictional" adventure story that Wilder writes about, which leads to the "real" adventure story that Wilder experiences. In a way, the opening hook acts in a similar manner to Mankiewicz's *News on the March* opening hook in *Citizen Kane* in that it presents in a summary fashion what will follow: the heroine has something the antagonist wants; she extricates herself from the dilemma, only to find another dilemma awaiting; when things look their bleakest, her hero comes to save her. So, just as Jesse rescued Angelina in the "fictional" story, Wilder is rescued by Colter in the "representational" story. As a matter of fact, there is a scene in the opening sequence in which we see not the characters of Angelina and Jesse on horseback riding toward each other, but Wilder and Jesse riding toward each other before the actors of Angelina and Jesse return in the final shot.

At approximately the tenth minute of the film, we get the introduction of the mysterious package from Colombia and that, in effect, opens

Pandora's box, since the trip to the jungles is the perilous journey Joan Wilder experiences. The battle, of course, is the battle for a treasure; the package she received contained a map indicating its whereabouts. Along with Colter, Wilder fights against the forces of evil—Ralph (Danny DeVito) and Ira (Zack Norman), as well as Zolo (Alfonso Arau), the latter of whom becomes the stereotypical Latino murderer. Wilder's exaltation is discovered in the ending, in which she's not only reconstituted herself but also found her man.

The revised 1983 script is rather ambiguous about what Joan looks like, but the film version is not ambiguous at all. At the outset, she is clearly a scattered, homely, self-effacing, shy woman who, presumably, puts all her romantic imagination into her novels and not into her life. But by the conclusion of her quest, she has made a major arc and has been totally transformed. By the end of the script, Joan and Colter (he is Colton in the script) have presumably gone their separate ways; Thomas writes, "He vanishes in the darkness. But Joan can't believe it. 'Jack Colton . . . damn it' " (104). In the following scene, Thomas writes that through the relationship with Jack, "there's a new spring in her walk, more assurance" (104), and the film bears that out. Not only has Wilder (she is Joan Charles in the script) changed psychologically, but her appearance also has changed dramatically: she has a new hairstyle, she wears cosmetics, and she dresses fashionably . . . all of these physical things have been altered from the opening sequence of scenes in which she is the exact opposite.

In the final scenes of the film, she turns the corner to her street and sees a huge yacht parked in front of her apartment. Atop the ship and wearing alligator boots (one of the last scenes with Colter has him fighting *mano a mano* with an alligator) is none other than Jack Colter. She climbs aboard, they speak romantically to each other, kiss, and as the film concludes, we see in a long shot the name of the yacht, Angelina, which not only acts as a refrain from the opening hook but presumably will act in a way to take them on to still new adventures together.

We can see that the opening and the ending have been unified. As a matter of fact, no other concluding scene could validate Aristotle's suggestion that the end should be linked to the beginning with inevitable certainty than the conclusion to *Romancing the Stone*. So here you can see how two categories, the comedy and the romance, have been joined and how the arc fits perfectly with Wilder's character, altering her from a rather ordinary and comely person to a rather extraordinary and beautiful one. So Thomas has completed the arc of the character, if not in the script version, then certainly by the end of the shooting script.

THE ROMANTIC/QUEST

Now if we were to look at romance as a category itself, without comedic overtones, one would be looking at it as a quest unto itself. Pure adventures tend to have their own phases, which are not entirely like those in romantic comedies. According to Frye, these phases are rather "cyclical" and include the following:

PHASE I

The myth of the birth of the hero, who often has mysterious origins.

PHASE II

The innocent youth of the hero, which is a story similar to Adam and Eve before the fall; the world is often a world of magic or desirable law, which tends to center on the youthful hero; the sexual barrier can also be included in this phase.

PHASE III

The normal quest theme of "good" versus "evil."

PHASE IV

The point at which the hero has to deal with the conflict between innocence and experience.

PHASE V

The point at which the story takes a reflective posture in which it contemplates experience in a rather idyllic if not nostalgic way.

PHASE VI

The final movement from an active to contemplative experience; the central image of such often being the "old man in the tower, the

lonely hermit absorbed in occult or magical studies"
(Frye, 198–202).

An excellent example of a purely romantic adventure in the manner that Frye describes is *The Name of the Rose*, a script apparently attempted by no fewer than four writers. The tale has the English Franciscan monk William Baskerville (the Scotsman Sean Connery) and his novice, Adso (Christian Slater), arriving at an Italian abbey in preparation for a conclave at which the future direction of the Catholic Church will be determined. A series of murders at the monastery alters the atmosphere for the conference and Baskerville, a devoted and observant semiotician, undertakes an investigation of the deaths. Here I take a look at the first few minutes of this quest and see how it might be adapted into the pattern of adventures that Frye talks about.

The myth of the birth of the hero, who often has mysterious origins.
The film opens in darkness, with the voice-over of Adso as an elderly man recollecting his innocent youth; when the story begins in earnest, we see Adso and Baskerville atop mules, tediously making their way to the monastery. Adso's origins are not that mysterious in that we know who his father is—the Baron of Melk—but we know little else about him. Of Baskerville's youth, we know nothing; however, we can see that this is a kind of separation phase for Adso much more than it is for Baskerville because it is a recollection of Adso's quest.

The innocent youth of the hero, which is a story similar to Adam and Eve before the fall; the world is often a world of magic or desirable law, which tends to center on the youthful hero; the sexual barrier can also be included in this phase.
Once inside the monastery, the heavy iron gates are closed and bolted, and a startled Adso finds himself more or less trapped within the walls of the monastery until the very end of the film. It is during this part of the film that he becomes initiated into the machinations of the monastery, which, to his way of thinking, must be paranormal indeed (i.e., magical and occult phenomena presumably occur there). Likewise, his entrance into the monastery is going to introduce him into the mysteries of the sexual experience with the girl who has no name.

91

The normal quest theme of "good" versus "evil."

For Frye, the normal quest theme involves a conflict between two main characters, a protagonist or hero, and an antagonist or enemy. Clearly, there is a conflict between Baskerville and Gui, who represents the Inquisition; however, by virtue of the fact that Baskerville is also Adso's mentor, Gui becomes his enemy as well and he participates in Gui's death.

The point at which the hero has to deal with the conflict between innocence versus experience.

In this phase, Adso is going to be initiated into the experiences of life as mediated by his metor, Baskerville. These experiences will challenge any preconceived notions of life and will ultimately climax with the discovery of how the monks have been murdered and finally conclude with Adso leaving the monastery. For Adso, the entire process has been an introduction into the world of experience and coterminous with that introduction is his inevitable loss of innocence.

Takes a reflective posture in which it contemplates experience in a rather idyllic if not nostalgic way.

The final movement from an active to contemplative experience; the central image of such often being the "old man in the tower, the lonely hermit absorbed in occult or magical studies" (Frye, 197–202).

This entire adventure culminates in the final movement of the film in which Adso, again in a voice-over as an old man, closes the circle by concluding that time in his active past while in his reflective, contemplative present. The connection between he and his master remains since he mentions that he's wearing a pair of glasses that Baskerville had given him. The allusion being that, perhaps, he now sees things through his master's eyes.

During the course of the film, Adso learns a great deal about himself and about life: he learns how to observe details; he loses his virginity (one of the longer scenes in the film); he learns the realities and horrors of death, and so on. One might assume that Baskerville is the hero of the story, and to some extent that's true because Connery's Baskerville is very similar in character to Connery's Bond (but without the bow tie) and he, too, learns something along the journey. However, the story begins and ends with Adso's recollections of that particular experience and the effect it had on his life, and Baskerville clearly plays the role of the mentor throughout that experience.

This story line also fits neatly into the Campbellian quest motif, with Adso's separation from his family (Baskerville says that he's in charge of Adso's education); his initiation into the mysteries of the monastery, the horrors of the Inquisition, and the struggles of adulthood; and his return as someone much different than the boy who began the journey. As a matter of fact, the last scene in the film leaves Adso with the rather adult choice of either staying with the girl he's "conquered" or continuing the journey with his mentor.

But within the first fifteen minutes of the film, some vital information has been established:

- Baskerville's visual abilities have been alluded to twice, and we actually see how observant he is.

- The Inquisition has been alluded to twice, and by virtue of that allusion one can conclude that it will make an appearance, which it does in the form of Gui, Baskerville's antagonist.

- Baskerville's heretical nature has been established, which will tie in with the Inquisition at some point.

- The notion of something evil has been established through the mysterious deaths at the monastery, which have been attributed to the devil.

- Baskerville's interest in scientific things has been established through his possession of such articles as a compass.

- Female perversion and male homosexuality have been alluded to.

- The conflict between the irrational and the rational, between church dogma and Aristotelian philosophy, has been established.

- The introduction of Adso's romantic interest has been established.

- Except for Gui himself, the major players in the story have been presented, including the murderer himself, Jorge Burgos.

So you see, we're beginning to find patterns in films as seemingly disparate as *Four Weddings and a Funeral* and *The Name of the Rose*. They fit into particular and rather conventional schemes that can be used to one's advantage in the process of trying to look for and implement specific story lines.

THE TRAGIC

From the quest adventure, we move to tragedy. Tragedy seems to be the easiest form to deal with, thanks mainly to what Aristotle has given us. We know that in romance the characters are still largely dreamlike, though they may appear real; in comedy their actions are meant to fit the demands of a happy ending. Whereas comedy tends to deal with characters in a social situation, Frye contends that tragedy tends to isolate individuals. "The tragic hero is typically on top of the wheel of fortune, halfway between human society on the ground and something greater in the sky . . . Tragic heroes are so much the highest points in their human landscape that they seem the inevitable conductors of the power about them, [like] great trees [which are] more likely to be struck by lightning than [is] a clump of grass" (Frye 1957, 207).

It's as if the character begins with everything going his or her way. He or she is sitting on top of the world; nothing could get better. Then something drastic happens. According to Frye, there are two reductive formulas that have often been used to explain tragedy. One is the theory that all tragedy exhibits the omnipotence of an external fate. The other is that the act that sets the tragic process going must be primarily a violation of moral law; in short, a fatal flaw (209–10). Like Oedipus, the protagonist only discovers at the end what has happened to him and recognizes the "determined shape of life he has created for himself, with an implicit comparison with the uncreated potential he has forsaken" (212).

As with the previous examples, we can see a crossover in that tragic comedies also prevail. A good example of this is the film *The Fisher King*, written by Richard LaGravenese. The film loosely adapts the Holy Grail quest by transposing it from Arthurian days to contemporary Manhattan. In it, the egotistical hero, Jack Lucas (Jeff Bridges), goes on a quest of self-redemption and love in which his entire being must be altered.

At the outset, we see that our hero begins on top of the wheel of fortune. Lucas is an arrogant, self-absorbed, marijuana-smoking, '60s-infatuated, radio jock totally consumed by his self-importance and his ability to say whatever he feels like saying with impunity. Lucas' complete lack of tact and respect for anything conventional invites one radio listener, Edwin Malnick, to take his advice literally, and Malnick returns to a local bourgeois bar called Babbitt's, takes out a shotgun, and massacres a restaurant full of yuppies. That arrogance becomes Lucas' fatal flaw. About seven and a half minutes into the film, Lucas accidentally discovers a live televised account showing the carnage created by Malnick and initiated by Lucas' rather flippant comments. The sequence ends at the ninth minute with Lucas, hand over mouth, uttering the futile words, "Oh, fuck."

Three years later, he is now a paranoid, alcoholic, suicidal video clerk working in a store owned and managed by Ann (Mercedes Ruehl), who has also been his devoted and loving caretaker as well as his sexual partner. After a disagreement in which Lucas tells Ann that he'd tell her anything "to get laid," he rushes out of the apartment amid a rainstorm and, after making friends with a Pinocchio puppet (to whom he recites excerpts from Nietzsche), ends up beneath what appears to be the Brooklyn Bridge. As he contemplates suicide once more, a couple of thugs attack him and pour gasoline on him. As they are almost ready to set him on fire, Parry, a.k.a. Henry Sagan (Robin Williams), shows up (at about the eighteenth minute) to save his life. Parry, who seems psychotic, befriends Lucas, takes him to his home—the boiler room of an apartment building—and tells him that the little people have told him that Lucas is the one to help him capture the Grail. At approximately the twenty-fifth minute, Parry utters the word *quest*, which segues into a newspaper photo that Parry possesses that shows a wealthy Manhattanite in his study standing next to what Parry imagines to be the Holy Grail resting on his bookshelf.

In a subsequent scene, at the thirtieth minute, the custodian of the apartment building tells Lucas that Parry is actually a former history professor named Henry Sagan who taught at Hunter College. He then goes on to say that Parry and his wife were in Babbitt's the night of the massacre and that Parry's wife was one of those murdered. Lucas suffers tremendously from guilt and tries to think of a way to assuage that guilt. In a curious circuit of events, he discovers that Parry is in love with a rather homely and scatterbrained publishing assistant, Lydia, whom Parry has stalked for months, and he and Ann contrive a way for them to get together. But Parry is also stalked by demons of his tragic past in the hallucinatory form of the "Red Knight," a surreal vision that constantly haunts him. After his date with Lydia, he is pursued by the knight until he too returns to the Brooklyn Bridge where, in a kind of hallucinatory state, he is beaten and slashed by the same two thugs who attempted to kill Lucas.

Feeling as if he's been revivified by what he's done for Parry, Lucas calls his former agent and tries to get his life back together, a move that greatly pleases Ann. However, Lucas explains to Ann that he wants to be alone, a confession that outrages her and presumably ends their relationship. Lucas then finds out about Parry, visits him in the hospital, and discovers that because of Parry's rather comatose state, he will be sent off to an institutionalized hospital to either regain consciousness or remain a vegetable.

At this point, things begin to improve for Lucas. His career somewhat resurrected, no longer drug-dependent, and in love with someone new, he has seemingly returned to the top of the wheel of fortune. But his experience with Parry and the other homeless men has altered his understanding of homelessness, and he returns to visit Parry, not entirely as a concerned friend, but as someone who is still guilt-ridden about what happened. As he screams at Parry, who lies comatose in his hospital bed, Lucas realizes that the only way to extinguish finally the guilt is to capture the "Grail" himself, and so he does.

In what one can consider a kind of Monty Pythonic attempt at capturing the trophy, Lucas returns to Parry's hospital and rests the trophy in Parry's hands. Miraculously, Parry awakens from his stupor, recognizes the "Grail," accepts his wife's death, and is able to move on. Likewise, Lucas returns to Ann, expresses his love for her, and the final scene of the film has Parry and Lucas lying nude in Central Park staring up at the stars. The film concludes with flashing lights and fireworks, a display that somehow undermines the artistic quest of the film.

The quest that Lucas takes inevitably leads to his own moral rediscovery. LaGravanese contends it's Jack's journey and "in creating Parry's character I wanted to create a fool—an innocent childlike character—who would open the door and lead Jack on his journey, because the story is really about Jack's [growth]" (Film Review Annual, 472). Likewise, "LaGravenese points out that it isn't attaining the Grail that helps Parry so much as it is Jack's gradual process of change" (Film Review Annual, 472). Certainly, Parry opens the door, but as he does so, he also assumes the role of Jack's mentor. But both of them have been altered through the course of the film. For Lucas, the act of questing for the "Grail" alters his arc from the arrogant, self-absorbed radio jock to the loving partner and friend; for Parry, receiving the "Grail" finally alters his state of being, eliminating the demon of the Red Knight and allowing him to move on with his life.

Like *Rocky*, *The Fisher King* script dated January 20, 1989, is not the same as the final cut of the film. There have been substantial changes, especially in the beginning of the film, which clearly tighten the focus on Lucas' arrogance. But there have been dynamic changes in subsequent scenes as well; too many, in fact, to catalog here, but despite many of the significant changes in the film, *The Fisher King* does comply with much of what Frye has talked about and it also relates to what Campbell has detailed.

Clearly, there is a quest, which is established as early as Parry's entry in the first act (on page 29 of the script) when he says, "the little people [have said] you're the one." He follows that further on with the line "I'm on a what you call a 'quest' " (LaGravenese 1989, 29). As Parry continues to talk to Lucas, he says, "And they [the little people] told me that I had been chosen for this special quest. You know what they want me to do, Jack? They want me to find the Holy Grail for them" (30).

Certainly, Parry acts as Lucas' mentor throughout the film: it is Parry who initiates the whole idea of the quest; it is Parry who recites the myth of the Fisher King; it is Parry who initiates Lucas into the underworld of the homeless; it is Parry who, like a transient Buddha, is constantly enlightening Lucas as to the real meaning of life. Clearly, too, there are the distinct divisions that Campbell has addressed: the separation (the fall from fortune); the initiation (into Parry's world); and the return (to his former career), but with the attendant feature of conscience. Also, the name "Sagan" is a collateral of the word *sage*, and who better than Sagan to save Lucas?

What differentiates the new Lucas from the old Lucas is conscience. His return to his former career is marked with a clearer understanding of who he is and what is important in life; and though it is not clear as to whether he remains in his old job subsequent to renewing his relationship with Ann, it is clear that he has come full circle and has completed the quest established in the first act of the film.

As is Campbell's scheme, Frye's scheme is exactly that—a scheme, a kind of operational structure to assist you in putting together your own story in a unified and cohesive way. But you should not be entirely dependent on trying to fit the story line exactly into the structure. For example, in *The Fisher King*, two of the main characters, Lucas and Ann, are introduced within the first 10 percent of the film, but Parry is not introduced until about 17 percent of the film (or approximately twenty minutes) has gone by, and his entrance tends to coincide with the movement from Act I to Act II when, at approximately the twenty-fifth minute, he mentions the word *quest*.

THE SATIRIC

From tragedy we move to satire. Frye indicates there are two things essential in satire:

1. wit or humor founded on fantasy or a sense of the grotesque or absurd
2. an object of attack (1957, 224)

But one of the key things we also find in satire is the notion of chaos, a kind of legitimized misrule and implied in that kind of chaotic element is the presence of someone who is in charge of that misrule—a kind of satirist, a fool, a clown, a trickster, one who deceives. What's significant about this kind of character is that she or he plays counterpoint to the ruling class or to the authority of the social order. These characters are heroic, but in a much different way than the heroes we find in any of the previous categories, since their heroism is founded upon a kind of abuse suffered because they tend to disrupt the natural order of things and undermine certain preconceived notions. The trickster "dupes others and is always duped himself. . . . At all times he is constrained to behave as he does from impulses over which he has no control. He knows neither good nor evil yet he is responsible for both. He possesses no values, moral or social, is at the mercy of his passions and appetites, yet through his actions all values come into being" (Radin 1969, ix).

So a character that is presented early in the film becomes a personification of that misrule and, in addition, establishes a leader of that misrule. In other words, the story establishes an opponent, whom the hero-fool can challenge. Likewise, we know that satire can be very close to the comedic. As Frye says, "the comic struggle of two societies, one normal and the other absurd, is reflected in the double focus of morality and fantasy" (1957, 224). So what we have is a form that is something both frivolous and serious. Like the other forms, the hero is on a quest, but the means to and the outcome of that quest can be quite different. Without going into the relationship between the fool and the Holy Grail, we can recognize that Parry, in *The Fisher King*, has many of the characteristics of the fool. Likewise, Paul Newman as Luke in *Cool Hand Luke* would fit into that category, as would Alan Bates in *King of Hearts*. But probably one of the best examples of this kind of trickster and the plot that accompanies him would be Jack Nicholson as McMurphy in *One Flew over the Cuckoo's Nest*.

What we find in this plot are comic-tragic elements, as opposed to comic-comic elements. As in *Cool Hand Luke*, the fool dies in this story even though his legend lives on. Therefore, the quest the fool is on is also a quest of discovery, but instead of ending happily, it ends semitragically. In general, satiric plots don't function on a linear basis. One would expect a chaotic situation to be rendered chaotically, but, in fact, disjunctive plots do not work in this kind of film, and though McMurphy is clearly the fool, the plot is not foolishly created.

The Bo Goldman script is brilliantly structured in such a way as to set a tone and a tempo that will inevitably be reorchestrated upon the entrance of McMurphy. It has a neat frame that begins and ends with the same shot, except the opening is at dawn and the closing is in the evening. Within the first three minutes, we are introduced to the setting— a hospital for those who appear to be mentally disturbed—the characters, the inmates, and their leader, Nurse Ratchet (Louise Fletcher). The setting is clearly one that elicits compliance, in that everyone there listens to and obeys Nurse Ratchet. Once those items have been established, things change. At approximately four minutes, McMurphy enters the hospital and immediately begins to play the fool. He watches everything very closely and at about the seventh minute meets the Chief, a gigantic man whom we believe to be both deaf and dumb. The inmates are playing pinochle, and that is a metaphor for the entire atmosphere in the hospital.

At about the eighth minute, McMurphy meets Dr. Spivey, and for almost the next six minutes we are introduced into the world of McMurphy through his history. We hear that he is belligerent, resentful in attitude, lazy, has a tendency to "fight and fuck too much," was sent from the work farm, had five arrests for assault, and has been accused of statutory rape. It is also clearly established that there is absolutely nothing wrong with his mind.

During the course of his stay, a number of changes occur that both infuriate Nurse Ratchet and undermine her power and authority. McMurphy quickly assimilates into the group and teaches the inmates how to play blackjack—using cards with naked women on them—instead of pinochle. He befriends the Chief; he refuses to take his medication; he commandeers a hospital bus and takes the inmates on a day out of fishing. In short, his injection into the system of the hospital is like the introduction of a disease. He slowly begins to gain the trust and admiration of the inmates and at about the thirty-eighth minute of the film, he bets he can pick up the sink, throw it through the wall, and escape. As the others look on, McMurphy tries with all his power to move the sink, but he can't because it's too heavy. As he leaves the bathroom, he says to the inmates, "I tried. At least I did that."

At about the fiftieth minute, McMurphy is brought back to talk to Dr. Spivey and others and explains to the physicians in attendance that the only problem he has is with Nurse Ratchet, who "ain't honest" and, according to McMurphy is "somethin' of a cunt." After a month of observation, no one can detect any mental illness in him. But it is at about the midpoint of the film, at approximately the sixty-third minute, that things really begin to change in the ward. As Nurse Ratchet conducts one of their minitherapy sessions, things get out of hand when Cheswick asks for his cigarettes and Ratchet won't give them to him. At that point, the patients begin to assert themselves, culminating with the usually passive Cheswick screaming at Ratchet: "Piss on your fucking rules, Miss Ratchet!" At that point, chaos begins. There's a free-for-all, and as the attendants come in to sort things out, there's a fistfight between McMurphy and the assistants. When the Chief sees McMurphy in trouble, he rushes to his aid. The scene ends with both of them being subdued.

The following scene opens with McMurphy, Chief, and Cheswick in chains. It is at this point that the Chief, feeling secure with McMurphy, says his first words, and McMurphy is overjoyed with the revelation because he wants to escape with the Chief. Though McMurphy is given electroshock therapy, which preconditions us for what will happen later, he is still the same McMurphy when he returns to the ward. The film really culminates in the last sequence of scenes, when McMurphy bribes the night watchman to let in some female friends of McMurphy's. The result is a drunken orgy, and the following morning Ratchet is completely out- raged at what happened. In the cleaning process, the attendants discover Billy, whom we know has had a problem relating to young women, in bed with one of McMurphy's friends. Ratchet says she'll have to tell Billy's mother, which sends him into a frenzy, and the scene culminates with Billy committing suicide and McMurphy, outraged at Ratchet, leaping onto her and trying to strangle her. Her life is spared only when one of the attendants finally pulls McMurphy off.

By the next scene, things are back to "normal" in the ward. Rumors sur- round McMurphy's whereabouts. Some say he's been beating up guards; some say he's "meek as a lamb." That evening the guards return McMurphy to the ward. Chief sees them put McMurphy into bed and once they've left he goes to him. He says to him that "now we can leave," then discovers that they've given McMurphy a lobotomy, turning the once vibrant and manic McMurphy into a vegetable. At that point, out of both love and respect for McMurphy, the Chief, realizing that McMurphy would never be the same, suffocates him. He then returns to the bathroom and does what McMurphy could not do: lift the sink, throw it through the wall, and escape. The film ends with the Chief running into the darkness to the sound of thumping Indian drums.

Clearly, the character of McMurphy and the plot of *One Flew over the Cuckoo's Nest* complies with what Frye has spoken of regarding satire. McMurphy represents that misrule about which Frye talks and the story line establishes an opponent (Nurse Ratchet), whom the hero-fool (McMurphy) can challenge.

So we've seen that these aspects of comedy, tragedy, romance, satire, and the quest, which all have their origins in narratives, can be applied quite effectively to screenwriting as well. What's important to recognize here is that script time is minimally variable and there is limited flexibil- ity in introducing your characters, in organizing the structure of the story line, and in appropriately dividing the acts. Because the time constraints are rigorous and ever-present, one has to keep those constraints in mind as well as one of the most important constraints—dialogue, a subject I'll talk about at length in the next chapter.

EXERCISE

Create a chart with five columns that include the following headings: comedy, romance, quest, tragedy, and satire. Then select one film that you feel fits into each of those categories. They can be old films or new films; it doesn't matter. Using the schemes I've discussed in the chapter, analyze those films, looking for the same markers Frye uses. Does the scheme hold? If not, how does it differ? In what aspects? Are there overlaps? Finally, fit your play into the scheme and see how it fits or doesn't fit.

WORKS CITED

Curtis, Richard. 1994. *Four Weddings and Funeral*. London: Corgi Books.

Film Review Annual. 1992. Englewood, NJ: Jerome S. Ozer Publisher.

Frye, Northrop. 1957. *Anatomy of Criticism: Four Essays*. Princeton, NJ: Princeton University Press.

LaGravanese, Richard. 1989. *The Fisher King*.

Radin, Paul. 1969. *The Trickster: A Study in American Indian Mythology*. New York: Greenwood Press.

Thomas, Diane. 1983. *Romancing the Stone*.

6
SCENE

Dialogue, or Look Who's Talking and Why

ONE OF THE MOST CURIOUS THINGS ABOUT BOOKS WRITTEN ON screenwriting is that the majority of them minimize or totally ignore dialogue. This exclusion is rather extraordinary since silent films ended in 1927, so for more than seventy years, we've been relying on dialogue to help carry the burden of the story line. Yet if one takes a look at the books being written on screenwriting, the number of pages devoted to dialogue runs from zero at the low end to about twenty at the high end, with the average being about six pages! Out of more than twenty books I reviewed, only two books actually had more than twenty pages devoted to dialogue, and only one went beyond thirty. That lack of attention to dialogue immediately begs the question: Why? One answer may be that the majority of the people writing books on screenwriting don't actually write screenplays or stage plays, so their notion of what good dialogue sounds like and, more important, what techniques are used to write good dialogue is extremely limited. I'm not saying that what any of these people have to say about dialogue isn't worth reading, only that there isn't much there to read.

We know that some of the best screenwriters actually began writing for the stage: Harold Pinter, David Mamet, Christopher Hampton, Tom Stoppard, and the late Steve Tesich, among others. Each of them has a clear understanding of what constitutes good dialogue and how best to write that dialogue. This chapter will attempt to present some techniques that they and others have used to write effective dialogue.

Let's try something different this time and begin with an exercise rather than end with one. The exercise is this: Choose two people, friends of yours, and have them begin talking to each other. You can either tape the conversation or just listen and take notes, but have them talk for a couple of minutes without necessarily giving them a topic. What are the key things you discover in hearing this ordinary conversation, and how might that apply to cinematic conversation? Usually what happens in this kind of situation is that you'll hear pauses, gaps of time in which nothing—or virtually nothing of any substance—is said, or you'll get a kind of rambling dialogue, staggered with clichés and empty words. That's exactly what you're looking for; we have to keep in mind that what you're dealing with in film dialogue isn't daily conversational speech but, as in character development, a simulacrum of daily speech. You're not presenting conversational dialogue but representing conversational dialogue.

To present that kind of dialogue effectively, one should keep in mind the notion of dialogous compromise. In other words, effective film dialogue must sound natural, even though it is totally and utterly contrived. Film dialogue is supposed to convey the sense of conversational speech even though it is much more structured than the meanderings of daily speech.

The tone of the dialogue has to sound conversational and, more importantly, nonacademic, unless the dialogue demands a kind of academic quality, as in certain scenes in *Good Will Hunting*. Yet screen dialogue does use those idiosyncratic things that we use in daily conversational speech such as pauses, stutters, tics, malaprops, slips of the tongue, rapid dialogue, repetition, and so on. The two main differences are:

- Those components of daily speech are compressed because of the prevailing limitations of time.
- The dialogue is constructed to reflect those limitations.

A character's sentences may be incomplete or interrupted, characters may mumble, evade, or exaggerate, but all of those things must be done within a context that propels the story line forward and makes the characters sound realistic. Ask yourself: How is that done? What's the key element in accomplishing that? Writing economically is the answer.

All of film writing should be economic, unless, of course, you're going to fund the film yourself, and then you can have your characters ramble on as long as they want, but if you're not financially solvent for that, effective dialogue is generally written sparsely, with speeches that are relatively short and succinct. That's not to say longer bits of dialogue should be eliminated. Clearly, what you write is scene-dependent and will function in terms of the context of what has been created; however, one should pay particular attention to how the dialogue is constructed so that unnecessary words are eliminated. We need only recall Rocky's words to his cornerman. In addition, dialogue should express who the character is and the character's mood and emotions in a particular scene. It should sound like the character and not like the writer, and it should take on the rhythm and expression of the character.

A failing of many novice scripts is often having characters go out of character not in action, but in dialogue. Granted, in *My Fair Lady*, there's a massive change in Audrey Hepburn's character both in temperament and speech, but even with that character she must be conditioned to be changeable. In other words, her accent, the register of her voice, and her delivery do not occur precipitously, but over a period of time so that by the end of the film we, as viewers, are convinced of the dialogous change even though realistically that change could not have happened so quickly. Ultimately, dialogue must achieve an effect of realism that will do several things either simultaneously or interdependently:

- present information dealing with the past; that is, the backstory
- define character by reflecting education, occupation, sociology, psychology, and so on
- engage the audience emotionally and/or elicit and sustain conflict
- propel the story line forward
- indicate movements of off-screen characters
- present the theme of the story
- preserve character and story line continuity

What we discover when working with these fundamental components of dialogue is that they tend to work in conjunction with and not independently of one another. In other words, most scenes will incorporate all or many of these things. But of the seven items I've listed there are four on which we need to focus, and those four together constitute the MADE rule of dialogue:

maintaining scenic continuity

advancing the story line

defining character

engaging emotionally and eliciting conflict

Now I'll discuss these items individually before I actually deal with some film examples.

DOES THE DIALOGUE MAINTAIN SCENIC CONTINUITY?

Questions to consider include, but are not limited to:

- What techniques are used in order to maintain the integrative function of the dialogue within the scene?

- How does one piece of dialogue synchronize with other dialogue to create a unified whole within the scene and, by extension, with other scenes?

- Does the dialogue sound like patchwork, with no unifying elements whatsoever?

- Does the repetitive use of words coordinate?

This area of scenic continuity is the area in which the dialogue, no matter how contrived it may be, most resembles conversational speech. The dialogue within each scene must link the beginning of the scene with the end of the scene for maximum effectiveness. Likewise, since each scene is codependent on every other scene, it's imperative that there be some kind of connecting device that links the dialogue from one scene to another.

DOES THE DIALOGUE ADVANCE THE STORY LINE?

Questions to consider include, but are not limited to:

- Does the dialogue assist in the flow of the story line?
- Does the dialogue digress?
- Does the dialogue give information that is not necessary to the story and can be given in another way (e.g., visually, graphically, aurally)?
- Does the dialogue give sufficient information to keep us informed of the vital things we need to know?

The ultimate question one must ask is this: Is the dialogue vital to the integrity of the story? Are there other ways of expressing what's being said and saving the dialogue for something else? We've seen in *Rocky* that Stallone includes props that effectively communicate things about Rocky's character that needn't be told through dialogue, thus utilizing the time devoted to dialogue for things that are more vital to the story line. There's absolutely no need to have Rocky say, for example, "I'm Catholic," or, "My favorite boxer was Rocky Marciano," or any number of other things that can be communicated visually and would not take away from dialogue time.

DOES THE DIALOGUE DEFINE CHARACTER?
Questions to consider include, but are not limited to:

- Does what the character says parallel who the character is? In other words, does the dialogue fit the character and help define who that character is?

- Does the dialogue sound like something the character would say or is it there for purposes other than defining character?

We know how Rocky speaks. No other character can speak quite like Rocky, or Ratso Rizzo, or Joe Buck, for that matter. We're not entirely interested in the manner in which he speaks, though the manner helps define character, but how and why he says what he says. Rocky's intonation will not alter by the end of the film, but the content of his dialogue will.

We know, for example, how Conrad (Timothy Hutton) initially speaks to Berger (Judd Hirsch) in *Ordinary People* and how his type of discourse, the manner in which he engages Berger, changes as his character arcs throughout the course of the film. At the beginning of the film, both language and position distance the two characters. Conrad is defensive, Berger inquisitive, and they sit at opposite sides of the room. By the end of the film, both language and position have altered. As Conrad becomes less defensive and begins to be more trusting, his dialogue alters, as does his physical relationship to Berger, culminating in the two of them embracing in their last scene together.

But what's critical in this regard is that the dialogue contributes to character development. Regardless of the seemingly irrelevant hamburger dialogue carried on between John Travolta's and Samuel Jackson's characters in *Pulp Fiction*, it says a great deal about their individual characters.

DOES THE DIALOGUE ENGAGE EMOTIONALLY AND ELICIT CONFLICT?

Questions to consider include, but are not limited to:

- Does the dialogue capture the audience's emotional attention?
- Does the dialogue allow for compelling interpersonal as well as intrapersonal conflict?

These are key aspects of quality dialogue because if a story deosn't engage an audience emotionally and elicit conflict, it is apt to become static and will lose an audience's interest. External dialogue, as opposed to internal (i.e., voice-over) or external monologue, is merely the dialogue between two characters that initiates some kind of conflict. As we'll see, in *The Graduate*, the scenes with Benjamin and Mrs. Robinson are often laden with conflict initiated by something one or the other has said. The internal conflict can be defined as the conflict that engages the character with him- or herself, based on the external dialogue. For example, the effect of Benjamin's conflicts with Mrs. Robinson contributes to a lot of his internal conflicts.

This applies to comedy writing as well as dramatic writing in the sense that not every line is going to be a punch line, but in order for the punch line to work, the dialogue must be structured in such a fashion as to lead up to that line effectively.

In *The Graduate*, which deals with both dramatic and comedic dialogue, the dialogue engages the characters and the audience emotionally and it elicits and maintains conflict even in its resolution.

Ultimately, the four major items I've just discussed must be conveyed through dialogue; it must:

Maintain

Advance

Define

Engage

But how, then, does a writer do that? If all cinema dialogue is contrived, what makes it sound so realistic? And, more important, how can it say all that needs to be said in the shortest possible space? It certainly isn't the kind of dialogue we hear in the classroom or on the streets or in the stores of our everyday life; that is, a kind of spontaneous, often focusless, speech. Good screenwriters utilize some very basic, but not easily learned, techniques when writing dialogue, and I'm going to focus on six specific devices, which you'll see not only in *The Graduate* but, if you pay close attention, in almost any well-written film. They include:

Question & Answer (Q&A)

Question/Statement Interrupt (QSI)

Question/Statement Lead (QSL)

Question/Question Lead (QQL)

Statement/Statement Lead (SSL)

Dialogue Linkage (DL)

I'll now go over each one of these categories one at a time:

QUESTION & ANSWER (Q&A)

This is just that: question and answer. A character asks a question that leads to an answer, but that answer functions on several levels; it should:

- advance the story line
- round out character
- give information vital to the scene
- give information vital to the story line

Q&A is the simplest technique used in dialogue writing and the one that is used most frequently. However, one of the main problems with it is that it can be overused, in which case one merely has a screenplay in which one character constantly asks questions while another character merely answers. This kind of Holmes and Watson type of dialogue often creates an imbalance that can result in the creation of static and rather predictable characters, if not predictable answers. To avoid that possibility we can incorporate the next device.

QUESTION/STATEMENT INTERRUPT (QSI)

QSI is a technique in which one character literally interrupts another character's dialogue (statement or question) to elaborate on the subject at hand or to change the direction of the dialogue. This, in effect, changes the direction of the scene but also gives information vital to the story line. This type of dialogue often occurs in daily speech, but in film dialogue it's clearly meant to work within the MADE structure.

QUESTION/STATEMENT LEAD (QSL)

QSL is dialogue that moves the focus of the dialogue from one subject to another. QSL differs from QSI in that the character doesn't interrupt another character but merely states something that redirects the dialogue to another focus. One character may pause for the other character to finish and then take up a new lead or maybe say something that appears to be irrelevant but has a particular importance that will change the dialogue's direction, and that direction will alter the focus of the scene.

QUESTION/QUESTION LEAD (QQL)
STATEMENT/STATEMENT LEAD (SSL)

QQL and SSL are variations of QSL, in that a question asked can be answered with another question or a statement made could be followed by another statement, but either action is done in order to advance the story line. Oftentimes we find that there is a linking device used to propel the dialogue forward.

Finally, each of these techniques can be used in conjunction with one other technique, namely, dialogue linkage.

DIALOGUE LINKAGE (DL)

DL is a technique of connecting one character's dialogue to another's by repeating certain words and/or phrases that will somehow unify the entire scene.

These techniques don't work in isolation but in combination with one another and at the same time they advance the four MADE items I've already addressed. With that in mind, we can take a detailed look at three scenes from *The Graduate* (1967) and analyze how Buck Henry utilizes those techniques so that the dialogue contributes not only to story line development but to character development as well.

I'll take them one at a time, but keep them all in mind:

- **Question & Answer**
- **Question/Statement Interrupt**
- **Question/Statement Lead**
- **Question/Question Lead**
- **Statement/Statement Lead**
- **Dialogue Linkage**

THE GRADUATE
Scenes 28–30

Scene 28

In the film version, there has been a transposition of certain segments of dialogue, which is not in the final-draft version of the script, dated March 29, 1967. In the film version, this particular scene opens with Benjamin (Dustin Hoffman) in his room, in darkness, with his head resting against a fish tank. Then the door opens and his father walks in. The position of the camera focuses first on Benjamin, in close-up, then as a tight-two shot with his father (William Daniels) cramping the frame. We then hear Mr. Braddock speaking, and the dialogue is basically the same as the master scene script until Scene 29.

What's significant in the dialogue is the way Henry uses the techniques I've mentioned. If we break the scene down into component parts, we actually have Mr. Braddock asking six questions to Ben's one.

Mr. Braddock opens with a question and follows it with a statement that establishes part of the story line, in that it addresses the fact there are guests downstairs waiting for Ben.

To Ben's question about wanting to be alone, which establishes Ben's lack of interest in visiting the guests, Mr. Braddock follows with additional information that they are all "our" (Mr. Braddock's) good friends who have known Ben since his birth.

At this point, Henry utilizes a combination of Q&A, QSI, and DL, all of which work to advance both character and story line.

For example, to Mr. Braddock's question "What is it, Ben?", Ben begins to answer, "I'm just . . .", but his father finishes the answer with " . . . worried." As Ben begins to answer, "Well . . .", Mr. Braddock turns it back into a question: "About what?" Benjamin answers, "I guess . . . about my future." His father then asks, "What about it?"

Then Benjamin starts to answer, "I don't know. I want it to be . . .", and his father both interrupts the statement and turns the statement into a question by asking, "To be what?", thus linking both dialogues with the words *to be* while advancing one of the key themes in the film: Benjamin's future. To answer his father's question about his future, Benjamin merely says, "Different." Different than what? Well, we find out, different than his father's or that of his father's generation.

Precisely at that point, Ben's mother walks in and fills the entire frame so that Benjamin is totally obliterated. In effect, in combination with Mr. Braddock, Mrs. Braddock suffocates both Benjamin's character and his dialogue; in other words, his voice. Her question about anything being wrong is answered by her husband, not Benjamin, and the two of them close the scene in dialogue by once again alluding to the guests and to the fact that it's a blessing to have so many "devoted friends." However, the devoted friends are not Benjamin's friends and that, in effect, prepares us for what's to follow.

Scenes 29–30

Scenes 29 and 30 have been altered in the film so that they continue the notion of suffocation that has been established in the opening scene. However, the scene is also divided into five precise segments, as Benjamin attempts to escape from his parents and his parent's friends.

- SEGMENT ONE: Benjamin walks downstairs, but he attempts to escape his parents' friends at the foot of the stairs by rushing to the front door, where he runs into . . .

- SEGMENT TWO: Mr. Loomis, who wants to know about the award he won. In an attempt to escape Mr. Loomis, he runs into . . .

- SEGMENT THREE: The three ladies at the foot of the stairs, who are so proud of him. Trying to avoid the three ladies, he is confronted by Mr. McQuire, who leads him outside . . .

- SEGMENT FOUR: Where Mr. McQuire utters the now-famous "plastics" line, after which Benjamin is confronted by yet another set of his parents' friends, which sends him rushing . . .

- SEGMENT FIVE: Back inside the house, where he rushes upstairs to seek refuge in his room once again, but as he does so, he passes Mrs. Robinson.

Those individual segments establish how the dramatic action of the scene is conveyed, but we need to take a look at how the dialogue advances that action and how it reinforces character.

Segment One. Certain key items are established in the dialogue vis-à-vis Ben's character. As he walks down the stairs, Mr. Carlson acknowledges in two statements that Benjamin:

- is an award-winning scholar
- has been given an Italian car (Alfa Romeo) as a graduation present

In a series of Q&As and SLs, the comment about the car moves to "picking up chicks and teenyboppers," to which Mrs. Carlson says, "I think Ben has gotten beyond the teenybopper stage," which, in fact, he has, as we'll soon find out. At that point, Benjamin works off the line about the Alfa Romeo to excuse himself because he'd "like to check something on the car for a minute." His attempt to escape the Carlsons concludes Segment One.

Segment Two. This begins his confrontation with Mr. Loomis. The dialogue continues to establish certain key elements as Mr. Loomis says, "Here's the track star himself. How are you, track star?" After Benjamin answers, Mr. Loomis follows it up with, "I want to hear all about that thing you won. That Hopperman award." Benjamin corrects him: "Helpingham." So the dialogue establishes two new bits of information:

- Benjamin is a track star.
- He won a Helpingham Award, which we can assume to be the award for scholarship.

Once again, in a brief Q&A and SL, we get specific information about Benjamin, the former of which is crucial, because several times in the film

Benjamin must rely on his running skills, the last time to save Elaine. The latter is also important in the bedroom scene with Mrs. Robinson. As Mr. Loomis goes off for a drink, Segment Two ends.

Segment Three. Here, three ladies, all of whom are picking at him, accost Benjamin. The combination of a tightly shot frame and the women doting on him and telling him how proud they are of him show how this only exacerbates his discomfort.

In addition to all of them being proud to excess, there's a Q&A that acts as a refrain from Scene 28—relating to Ben's future—when Lady Three asks, "What are you going to do now?" Benjamin takes the question literally and says, "I was going to go upstairs." She corrects him and says, "No—I meant with your future." Lady Two adds, "With your life," and he replies, "That's a little hard to say." At exactly that line, Mr. McQuire enters, excuses both of them from the consort of ladies, and escorts Ben outside, thus ending Segment 3.

Segment Four. In this segment, there is a Q&A with Mr. McQuire uttering the now-famous line "Plastics." Benjamin responds, "Exactly how do you mean?" Mr. McQuire answers, "There is a great future in plastics." So the DL between one's future and plastics is meant to satisfy him. As McQuire leaves and Ben is confronted with yet another group of his parent's friends, he excuses himself and rushes back into the house. This escape ends Segment Four.

Segment Five. In this segment, Benjamin runs through the living room, passing Mrs. Robinson (Ann Bancroft, this is not in the master scene script), and running upstairs. At this point we get the off-camera dialogue from Mrs. Terhune that was written for the early part of the scene. Through this dialogue we hear about Benjamin's college recognitions, which continues to round out his character, as he flees the constrictions brought about by his parents and their friends and rushes to his bedroom.

Scene Thirty-One

After Benjamin slams the door, he walks to the window and looks out at the people standing outside the patio, all of whom, from his point of view, look as if they too are in a fish tank.

So by the end of these four scenes, we should return to the questions I posed earlier. Has the dialogue:

1. Maintained continuity?
2. Advanced the story line?
3. Defined character?
4. Elicited conflict?

In short, the answer is yes to all four questions, and it's important to note that no bit of dialogue ever exceeds four lines. So, not only has the dialogue accomplished all of its tasks, but it has also maintained precision and brevity.

Scenes 55–61

We've now got Benjamin deeply involved in his quest. Mrs. Robinson has extended him a sexual invitation, in the nude, and he's now acted on it by calling her up. We can pick up with the story line at their first hotel assignation.

Scene 55

This is an excellent scene in terms of how the dialogue continues to maintain continuity, advance the story line, define character, and elicit conflict.

Here we get not only the usual Q&A (as in Scene 28) but also the repetition of certain words or phrases, which links each dialogue. In the scene with the clerk (Buck Henry), Benjamin nervously repeats that he wants a room; Henry answers, "Single or double?" and we get the "single" link.

As he mistakenly signs his own name, then signs an alias, the clerk asks, "Any luggage . . . Mr. Gladstone?" Because the clerk states the name, we now know Benjamin's alias so that in any future scenes there won't be any confusion and it will add to the comedic moment. It also plays on the word *luggage* and that, of course, extends the absurdity of the situation when Benjamin admits that the only luggage he has in the car is actually a toothbrush and that he can play on that word again to avoid any confrontations with the porter.

Scenes 56–58

These scenes involve the phone conversation that Benjamin has with Mrs. Robinson. They are beautifully constructed in that the Q&A is comical and the dialogue economic, continuing to work primarily on developing Benjamin's character as someone who is extremely inept at this kind of thing. This idea culminates in the closure of the scene, when Mrs. Robinson asks, "Isn't there something you want to tell me?" Benjamin uses a question to answer the question and also plays off the link, "To tell you?", to which she says, "Yes." Benjamin then begins to tell her how much he appreciates what she's doing for him, when she says, "The number." "What?" he asks. "The room number, Benjamin. I think you should tell me that." Which he does.

The scene then coalesces with the next scene that not only comments once again on the toothbrush absurdity (as Benjamin passes the clerk, he pats his breast pocket and says to the clerk that he's got his toothbrush) but also continues to develop Benjamin's character, leading to a critical moment in Scene 61.

Scene 61

The remarkable thing about the dialogue in this scene is how well it does all four things at the same time.

- It maintains continuity.
- It advances the story line.
- It continues to develop character (not only Benjamin's but Mrs. Bobinson's).
- Most important, it elicits conflict.

I like to look at this scene as a scene of discovery, as a quest scene or initiation scene. As in an earlier scene, it opens in the dark and Benjamin would like it to continue in the dark, but Mrs. Robinson always turns on the lights, both literally and metaphorically. But the scene is clearly divided into three segments.

Segment One. Here Benjamin reacts to Mrs. Robinson's commands; in the early part of the scene she's entirely in control. For example, she says:

- "Watch me get undressed."
- "Get me a hanger."
- "Unzip my dress."

All of these commands continue to accent Benjamin's anxiety and inexperience in these situations. They also show his obedience to Mrs.

Robinson, illustrated by how he stands around with his arms folded. This reactive part continues until she takes off her blouse, leading into the next segment.

Segment Two. This begins with Benjamin feeling her breast and then having second thoughts about what he's doing, bringing into conflict his feelings of sexual desire versus his sense of morality. The second segment increases his anxiety and ends when Benjamin asks if she wants to do something else, such as go to a movie; her pause leads to the last segment.

Segment Three. Mrs. Robinson does not answer his question, but pauses and poses another, more critical question, which redirects the focus of the discussion, by attacking his virility: "Benjamin, is this your first time?" After all, she didn't come to the hotel to chat, nor to go to the movies; she came to have sex with a younger man. It's here that the dialogue does such a brilliant job of eliciting conflict by integrating the techniques of Q&A, statement interrupt, and dialogue link.

Beginning on page 53 of the script, Mrs. Robinson asks Benjamin if it's his first time. He answers with a question—"What?"—to which she replies with a question—"It is isn't it?" Then answers the question herself, "It *is* your first time."

So she emphasizes the notion of it being his first time. He responds that it's really a laugh, ha ha, but she continues on the attack by asking yet another question: "You can admit that can't you?", seeking a confession no virile, young, graduate male would care to make, especially to an older woman.

From that point on, we get a marvelous bit of parallel monologue in which Mrs. Robinson essentially ignores Benjamin's protestations as he attempts to defend himself, resulting in the exact thing she wanted to happen in the first place, that is, the excitation of his sexual desire. The clinching and winning argument for her is to emphasize that he's "inadequate," which she repeats twice almost in passing, and he screams the word as if it were the ultimate insult. Her pause allows her to feign getting dressed, to which Ben yells: "Don't move!"—a command that runs exactly counter to how the dialogue in the scene began, with Mrs. Robinson giving the orders.

So we see how the scene itself has moved in a particular arc from Benjamin's acquiescent, reactive position to an active, assertive posture, all mediated by Mrs. Robinson's provoking. The dialogue, then, reflects that direction. His actions, coupled with his dialogue, direct the scene to its natural conclusion and continue to develop character and story, initiate conflict, and maintain continuity.

Let's take a look at one more extended example that exhibits all of these things again; this time I want you to be aware of the kinds of techniques I've been talking about.

Scene 91

This scene has been greatly revised. Originally it was an eighteen-page scene, but it was cut to about ten pages. It's an excellent scene to analyze not only in terms of technique but also to see what was removed in order to make the techniques work more effectively. The first major difference is that the final draft of the script has Benjamin and Mrs. Robinson getting undressed while carrying on the dialogue before they get into bed, whereas the film has them already in bed before the dialogue begins. There may be a couple reasons for that revision, which I discuss in the following sections.

Story Line

The reason they're in the hotel in the first place is to have sex, so why not eliminate anything within the scene that might impede the achievement of that goal? Having them already in bed not only accomplishes that but also emphasizes how distant they are, given the conclusion of the scene.

Character

The revision creates a more intimate scene than having them undress apart from each other, and that intimacy allows the camera to focus on the two lovers alone and concentrate entirely on their dialogue. In addition, because the evolution of the scene will demand that they be next to each other, having them in bed makes that movement easier. It also works into the conclusion of the scene, in which they are no longer together, but dress and undress apart.

There have been major revisions in the scene by eliminating dialogue that did not really contribute to the flow of the story. In the final script version, there are approximately eleven topic areas, some of which take up significantly more time than others. I'm going to take a look at these areas and see how they've been revised.

Final Script Topic Divisions

1. dialogue about talking
2. dialogue about undressing
3. dialogue about art
4. dialogue about undressing again
5. dialogue about daily life/discussion about husband
6. dialogue about leaving the house
7. dialogue about the history of her marriage
8. dialogue about her pregnancy
9. dialogue about Elaine/conception
10. dialogue about Elaine/dating
11. dialogue about Elaine/conflict

Of these eleven areas within the script, a large portion is devoted both to the discussion of undressing and to Mrs. Robinson's husband (see divisions 5–8). However, in the film version the entire dialogue devoted to the act of undressing and the majority of the dialogue about her husband have been eliminated and replaced by one allusion to her husband, thus reducing the topic areas to five, or less than half of the original number, which accounts for the difference in script length. In the final film version, we have the following:

Film Version Topic Divisions

1. dialogue about talking/allusion to art
2. dialogue about art/daily life/Mr. Robinson/Elaine's birth
3. dialogue reprise of art/Elaine's birth
4. dialogue about Elaine/dating
5. dialogue about Elaine/conflict/resolution

Divisions 3–5 remain the same primarily because that dialogue is the most fundamentally conflictual. Actually, the entire scene has really been structured to lead up to one major conflict about Elaine Robinson (Katherine Ross), since it will be the physical introduction of Elaine that will dramatically alter the direction of the story line.

With that information as a point of departure, I'll now look at what Henry has done in terms of technique vis-à-vis the five primary divisions of the scene.

Dialogue about talking/allusion to art. Ben opens with the statement that all they ever do is "leap into bed together," to which Mrs. Robinson replies with a question: "Are you tired of it?" Ben answers with a statement/question lead: "No, but do you think we could liven it up with a few words now and then?" She answers with a question lead: "Well, what do you want to talk about?" She suggests that they could talk about his college experiences, but when he asks her to think of another topic, she replies, "Art," which leads to the next division.

Dialogue about art/daily life/Mr. Robinson/Elaine's birth. Ben asks her to "start it off," and she links to his dialogue by repeating, "You start it off," alleging she knows nothing. Ben then asks four quick questions related to art, which we know he can do because he's an award-winning scholar, but she replies indifferently. Insistent on conversing, he asks another question: "What did you do today?", which redirects the dialogue from art to daily life.

She says, "I got up. I fixed breakfast for my husband," and that takes us in another direction. At this point, Benjamin becomes the interrogator and he asks all the questions about their marriage. For example, Benjamin asks the question "Well, then, why did you marry him?" She asks if he can guess; he can't. She says he should try harder, leading him to ask if she had to. Mrs. Robinson responds by saying he shouldn't say anything to Elaine. With the mention of Elaine, the focus of the dialogue then takes another direction.

Dialogue reprise of art/Elaine's birth. Benjamin asks questions about the past that clarify the pregnancy issue. First he asks if her husband were a student at the time, then he asks if she were a student as well. She affirms. He then asks what her major was, prompting Mrs. Robinson to ask why he's asking all those questions. He says he's interested, then re-asks the question about her major, to which she replies, "Art." That puzzles Benjamin and he adds that she probably lost interest in art over the years. She responds, "Kind of."

So through a series of questions and answers, Benjamin discovers her major and we get the reprise of art and a clearer understanding of Mrs. Robinson's character. Ben continues asking questions about the pregnancy, leading off by asking how it happened. She seems puzzled by the question and that prompts Benjamin to clarify; he wonders about how it happened between them. She admits that it took place in Mr. Robinson's car, which prompts Benjamin to ask what kind of car it was. Mrs. Robinson is again puzzled by the question, so Benjamin repeats it. She can't believe the topic of conversation, but Benjamin presses her to remember the make. She responds that it was a Ford.

BEN: A Ford! A Ford! Goddammit, that's great! A Ford!

That's enough chatter for Mrs. Robinson, who wants to get back to the "action at hand," so when Benjamin says that Elaine was conceived in the backseat of a Ford, that particular line of questioning leads us in another direction, which really becomes the focus of the scene when Mrs. Robinson asks Benjamin not to talk about Elaine.

In a brilliant use of a statement converted into a question lead by repeating the same phrase, the entire direction of the scene shifts to the fourth division.

Dialogue about Elaine/dating. One sees that Ben has rarely made a statement. All his questions have been question leads, prompting for the make of the car, which becomes the focus of the dialogue and allows Benjamin to make the statement lead about how Elaine got her start in a Ford.

When Benjamin mentions Elaine's name, it prompts Mrs. Robinson to say, "Don't talk about Elaine" (a provocation), and moves Benjamin to link on her dialogue, which, through yet another and extensive series of questions and answers, moves him to make the fatal comment about taking Elaine on a date. To this, Mrs. Robinson violently reacts, leading to the last division.

Dialogue about Elaine/conflict/resolution. This is the final phase of the scene. Once again Benjamin poses all the questions for Mrs. Robinson to answer in relation to why she doesn't want Benjamin to take Elaine out. Benjamin suggests that it's because "he's not good enough," to which she responds, "Yes." Benjamin becomes angry, which is significant because it is the first time we actually see his anger sustained. His character now is in stark contrast to the character we met at the beginning of the affair. Though Benjamin is being initiated into the role of an adult, Mrs. Robinson is still a formidable adversary and she defuses his anger by altering what she just said about him, apologizing if "that's the impression you got" and rephrasing it to mean they wouldn't get along. Once again she has regained his allegiance and he changes his mind about leaving. However, Mrs. Robinson begins again by asking Ben to promise never to take Elaine out. He gets upset and responds that the idea never really occurred to him. But that's not enough for Mrs. Robinson, who wants Benjamin to give her his word that he won't, leading to the final dialogue in the scene in which Mrs. Robinson demands that Benjamin promise her.

BEN: All right, for Christ's sake. I promise I will never take out Elaine Robinson.
MRS. ROBINSON: Thank you . . . Benjamin—
BEN: Let's not talk about it. Let's not talk at all.

And with this statement, the scene closes on his promise and their silent undressing, which is in direct contrast to the opening of the scene that was predicated on the two of them talking.

If we break down the scene into its component parts, we'll find the following:

- Benjamin asks thirty-nine questions.
- Mrs. Robinson asks seventeen.
- Benjamin makes thirty-nine statements.
- Mrs. Robinson makes fifty statements.

From that total, we can then see how the dialogue links are dispersed.

Remembering that the dialogue link is the technique that is used to unify independent dialogues and propel the story line forward through the use of repetitive words or phrases, I came up with these results:

Dispersal of Dialogue Links

dialogue links related to art	9x
dialogue links related to Mr. Robinson	4x
dialogue links related to Elaine	4x
dialogue links related to being a student	2x
dialogue links related to Mrs. Robinson's major	2x
dialogue links related to the Ford	6x

dialogue links related to telling	2x
dialogue links related to hearing reasons	2x
dialogue links related to not being good enough	2x
dialogue links related to being sick and disgusting	4x
dialogue links related to acting hurt	2x
dialogue links related to her daughter	2x
dialogue links related to promises	3x
	44 Links

One can see how, just by looking at the number of links alone, one can evaluate the direction of the scene and how the dialogue is not only advancing the story line but developing character and eliciting conflict all in a very fluid yet unified way. The scene begins with questions about Mrs. Robinson and her background, redirects to Elaine, and then couples Elaine and Benjamin by the end of the scene, thus preparing the reader for what's to transpire in upcoming scenes.

As I mentioned at the outset of the chapter, this dialogue clearly sounds conversational, but, in fact, it is totally contrived and includes all the techniques I mentioned. This approach is not unique to Henry. If we were to take films from some of the better screenwriters, such as Steve Tesich (*Breaking Away*), Richard LaGravenese (*The Fisher King*), and Alvin Sargent (*Ordinary People*), we would see the same techniques being used. In short, they are the techniques that make for the best and most precise kind of film dialogue. As a matter of fact, we can use an excerpt from *Rocky* (1976) to see how Stallone managed with the dialogue.

The scene I use here is the scene in which Rocky discovers that his equipment has been put on "skid row," meaning he's essentially been tossed out of the gym. Outraged, he goes to Mickey (Burgess Meredith) to complain as Mick is watching Dipper, another fighter.

ROCKY: Howya feelin' today?
MICK: What?
ROCKY: I said howya feelin' today?
MICK: What are you a doctor or somethin?
ROCKY: You got a problem today.

MICK: Never mind my problem. What's your problem?
ROCKY: My problem is I've been talkin to your man Michael and I wanna know how come I've been put outta my locker.
MICK: Because Dipper needed it. Dipper's a contender. He's a climber. You know what you are?
ROCKY; What?
MICK: You're a tomata.
ROCKY: A tomata.

Mick then asks Rocky if he fought recently and Rocky says he did. Mick asks whom he beat and Rocky tells him Spider Rico. Mick spits on the floor.

MICK: He's a bum.
ROCKY: You think everybody I fight is a bum.
MICK: Well ain't they? You got heart but you fight like a goddamn ape. The only thing special about you is that you never got your nose busted so leave it that way nice and pretty and what's left of your mind.

If we ignore the opening exclamatory sentences, we can begin with Mick asking what Rocky wants. Rocky answers with a question, which Mick answers with a question, which allows Rocky to repeat the question and, at the same time, link the phrase "howya feelin' today?" So we have one question, an answer as a question lead, and another question, followed by another answer as a question lead.

Mick then asks a question about whether Rocky is a "doctor or some-thin' " but instead of answering, Rocky redirects the focus of the dialogue by asking if Mick has a problem today. Mick answers to never mind about his problem, but he asks about Rocky's problem. Rocky answers that he wants to know why's he's been kicked out of his locker. So we have a question, which is answered with a question lead that is answered by another question, which is answered by a statement, and all four exchanges are linked by the word *problem*.

Mick answers that he's been kicked out because "Dipper needed it" because Dipper is a contender, and that naturally leads to Mick's question to Rocky: "You know what you are?" Rocky asks, "What?" Mick answers, "A tomata." Rocky links on the word *tomata*, which prompts Mick to make a statement about running a gym not a soup kitchen. He then asks Rocky if he fought the night before. Rocky affirms. Mick asks if he won. Rocky affirms. Mick asks whom he fought. Rocky says, "Spider Rico." Mick answers that he's a bum. Rocky responds that Mick thinks everyone he fights is a bum. So we have the following: a question followed by an answer that is another question, both of which are linked by the word *tomata*. Then we get three rapid Q&As with two statement leads linked by the word *bum*, which not only indicates what Mick thinks of Rocky but continues the bum theme established in the first scene of the film.

Coming off of the bum link, Mick asks another question: "Ain't they?" and then answers the question himself with the statement lead that the only thing special about Rocky is that he's never had his nose broken, a statement that prepares us for the eventuality that it will be broken.

As Rocky starts to leave, he says he's going to take a steam because he fought well the night before and "you [Mick] shoulda' seen me," then he repeats the same thing to Dipper. Mick responds with a question about whether Rocky has ever considered "retirin'." Rocky answers "no" and that prompts Mick to say, "You think about it [retirin']." The scene closes with Dipper commenting that he digs Rocky's locker, which is repeated by Mick, and that exchange effectively ends the dialogue in the scene.

In terms of links, what we see in this brief exchange is the following:

Howya' feelin' today?	2x
problem	4x
Dipper	2x
tomata	2x
win/won	2x
bum	2x
shoulda seen me	2x
think about/retirin'	2x
I dig your locker	2x
	20 Links

In just this brief scene, Stallone has used about twenty links to maintain the flow of the dialogue and to emphasize some key things in relation to plot and character. It clearly establishes the conflict between Rocky and Mick, which, in some fashion, will have to be resolved; it maintains the bum theme established earlier in the film; it presents the vital information that Rocky has never had his nose broken; and, lastly, it reemphasizes Rocky's conflict with himself and his self-esteem. In the film version there is the added component related to Rocky's "job," which is not included in the script version.

But if you think this kind of dialogue is purely for standard or prototypical Hollywood-type films, let's take an example from a scene that is totally unlike the standard Hollywood-type film: *Pulp Fiction*. The key scene to work with here is the scene with Mia (Uma Thurman) and Vincent (John Travolta) at Jack Rabbit Slim's restaurant. The scene itself is approximately ten minutes in length, but because of the way in which the dialogue is structured it moves extremely fast and both advances the story line and rounds out each character. The scene can be broken down into nine individual dialogue segments, all of which are linked with a common theme: sharing. Though there are some alterations between the script and the film versions, they are somewhat minor and don't detract from the dialogous techniques Tarantino is using. The divisions include:

1. ordering/food and drink
2. cigarettes
3. acting
4. jokes
5. laughter
6. milk shakes
7. silence
8. Marilyn Monroe
9. Antwan

The dialogue opens with Vincent and Mia being waited on by a Buddy Holly impersonator, who asks if he can take their order. Vincent asks for the Douglas Sirk steak, to which Buddy asks if he wants that burned or "bloody as hell." Vincent repeats the phrase. Mia orders the Durwood

Kirby burger, bloody, and a "five-dollar shake." Buddy links off "shake" by asking if she wants it "Martin and Lewis or Amos and Andy." She links with "Martin and Lewis." Vincent follows by asking if she just ordered a shake that costs five dollars, she says yes, and he repeats the question: "A shake?" Then he adds, as if questioning reason, whether it just has milk and ice cream in it. She affirms. He then re-asks Buddy about it costing five dollars and Buddy reaffirms. Puzzled, he asks if there's any alcohol in it and Buddy says no.

By the end of Segment One there have been eight questions asked and nine statements made and there have been no fewer than eight links:

bloody	3x
five-dollar shake	3x
Martin and Lewis	2x
	8 Links

Segment Two begins with Mia asking Vincent what he thinks of Jack Rabbit Slim's. He answers, then proceeds to roll himself a cigarette, to which she asks him what he's doing because she thinks he's rolling marijuana. He says he's just rolling a cigarette because it's only tobacco he's rolling. She asks, "will you roll me one, cowboy?" He responds that she can have the one he's rolling and calls her "cowgirl," thus linking off the "cowboy" line. Brief as this segment is, we get four questions, four answers, one major link, "cowboy-cowgirl," and two statements that close the segment, but the unifying element in the dialogue is the act of sharing. The cigarette Vincent rolled was meant for him, but he gave it to her, for which she thanks him. That dialogue closes the segment, allowing Mia to redirect the dialogue in another direction that leads to Segment Three.

Segment Three opens with Mia stating that Marsellus told her that Vincent just came back from Amsterdam. He says yes and immediately redirects the course of the dialogue by changing the subject when he "asks" in a statement, "I heard you did a pilot." She replies it was her fifteen minutes of fame, with the "minutes" alluding to the "pilot." Vincent asks her what it was and she replies that it was a show about a handful of female secret investigators called "Fox Force Five," thus the word *it* links the dialogues.

Vincent asks, "What?" as if he didn't hear her correctly, which allows her to restate the name of the program, "Fox Force Five," then clarify what that meant in terms of what the characters did. She mentions that they each had "special skills," which allows Vincent to ask what her specialty was. She responds, "Knives," repeats the word *knife* twice in describing what her character did, and adds that she was also an acrobat who knew a lot of old vaudeville jokes that her grandfather had told her when she was a kid. She then ends her dialogue with the allusion to the fact she would have told a joke in each episode if the show were picked up. That statement allows Vincent to link off her dialogue by asking whether she remembers anything from the script concerning "jokes." That question concludes Segment Three and links to Segment Four, and we can see certain linking devices at work:

"Pilot" links to her "fifteen minutes" [of fame].

"It" links to what the show was, namely, a pilot.

"Fox Force Five" links to the name of the show.

"Special skills" links to the "specialty" the character had in the show.

"Knives" links to "knife," which links to "acrobat," which links to "old jokes," prompts Vincent's question.

So we get the following links:

it	2**x**
Fox Force Five	2**x**
special/ty	2**x**
knives/knife	3**x**
old joke(s)/joke	3**x**
	12 Links

In summary, we get one statement lead, which initiates a redirected statement lead, followed by four questions and four answers, all of which include twelve links.

Segment Five actually begins with Vincent's question about the joke, which prompts Mia to say she could only tell one since the program wasn't picked up. Vincent wants to hear it, but she says "it" was pretty "corny," to which Vincent replies that she should tell him. Mia responds that he wouldn't like "it" and she'll be embarrassed. Vincent links off the "it" by following with the promise that he won't laugh. She laughs, then says: "That's what I'm afraid of." Vincent follows by linking with that wasn't what he meant to say and continues with, "I meant I wouldn't laugh at you." She replies, "That's not what you said," and she won't tell him the joke. The segment ends with Vincent saying that he got gypped. So we can see the following linking devices at work:

"one" links with "it's really corny"

which links with "you won't like it"

which links with "you told it in front of fifty million people"

"won't laugh" links with "that's what I'm afraid of"

which links with "that's not what I meant"

which links with "I meant I wouldn't laugh"

which leads to not telling the joke

which ends the segment

The number of links includes:

it('s)	3x
that's	3x
meant	2x
laugh	2x
	10 Links

The dialogue ends with Buddy returning with the drinks, which initiates Segment Six, the milk shake segment. Mia sips the shake, prompting Vincent to ask if he could have a taste since he's still not sure what a five-dollar shake must taste like. She says he can use her straw since she doesn't have "kooties." He responds that it's possible that he might have them (i.e., kooties). But she responds, "Kooties I can handle." He sips and says, "That's a pretty fuckin' good milk shake." She affirms. "I don't know if it's worth five dollars, but it's pretty fuckin' good." In this segment we have one question, one answer, a statement lead (about kooties), and a refrain from Segment One related to the shakes. In terms of links, we have the following:

five-dollar (shake)	2x
kooties	2x
pretty fuckin' good	2x
	6 Links

What's beginning to happen here is that the two of them are becoming closer to each other and their intimacy is reflective of who their characters are.

Segment Seven begins with the first "uncomfortable silence," which Mia breaks by asking the question "Don't you hate that?" Vincent answers with the question "What?" Mia responds with, "Uncomfortable silences." Then she asks why it's necessary to yak about nonsense "in order to be comfortable." Vincent doesn't know. She replies that's when you know you've found someone special—when two people can "comfortably share silence." Vincent says that they're not "there yet," which presupposes that they may be there at some time. Mia says she's going to powder her nose and leaves Vincent to think about "something to say." So we get three questions, one answer, and a statement lead. The key links we get are:

un/comfortable/comfortably	3x
silence(s)	2x
	5 Links

So Tarantino used five links in a very brief period of time. At this point, Mia leaves, but a number of key things have been established between them, not the least of which is their growing interest in each other.

After Mia returns from the rest room, where she's snorted a line of coke, the dialogue continues essentially in the same manner as it ended in the previous scene. Mia opens with a rhetorical question about how good it is to return from the bathroom with your food waiting for you and Vincent responds with a comment about Buddy Holly's poor waitering skills, suggesting that "we shoulda' sat in Marilyn Monroe's section." She works off the Monroe allusion by saying, "Which one? There's two Marilyn Monroes." That sets up a kind of minor disagreement as he disagrees about how many Monroes there actually are. Vincent tells her that one of them is actually Mamie Van Doren, not Marilyn Monroe, and that because he doesn't see Jayne Mansfield she must have the night off. Mia comments on how smart he is to distinguish between Monroe and Van Doren, which prompts Vincent to reply that he has his "moments."

So we've got one question, to which there is one answer, one statement lead about Monroe, and another statement lead about Vincent's "smartness." In terms of links, we have three, all of which work off "Monroe."

Mia then asks him if he thought of "something" to talk about, which is a reprise of the line she concluded with before she went to the rest room. He replies that there's "something" he wanted to discuss with her, thus working off the "something" line. Her response includes the line "This sounds like you actually have something to say," which continues to link on the repetition of the word *something*. He says, "Only if you promise not to get offended," to which she double links with, "You can't promise something like that . . . and my natural response could be to be offended. Then, through no fault of my own, I would've broken my promise." So she's continued the dialogue by accenting the two links: "promise" and "offended."

Vincent then says, "Then let's just forget it," to which she links with, "Trying to forget anything as intriguing as this would be an exercise in futility." "Is that a fact?" he asks; she nods. Vincent then moves the dialogue in another direction by asking about what happened to Antwan. She answers with a question: "Who's Antwan?" Vincent answers, "Tony Rocky Horror." She replies, "He fell out of a window." Vincent answers that that would be one way of looking at it and then posits the possibility that he was thrown out by Marsellus "because of you." Mia then repeats the question he gave earlier, thus linking the two, by asking, "Is that a fact?" He answers that it was something he heard. She asks another question: "Who told you?" He answers, "They." The next three exchanges include the "they" link, finally leading to Vincent mentioning that Rocky Horror gave her a foot massage. "And?" she asks. "No and; that's it," he answers. She asks another question: "You heard Marsellus threw Rocky Horror out of a four-story window because he massaged my feet?" "Yeah," he answers. "And you believed that?" Vincent responds that at the time it seemed "reasonable," to which she links off the word *reasonable* by both repeating the line about Marsellus throwing Rocky Horror out of the window and turning it into a question: "Marsellus throwing Tony out of a four-story window for giving me a foot massage seemed reasonable?" Vincent responds that he thought it was "excessive," but "Marsellus is very protective of you," to which Mia links by saying, "A husband being protective of his wife is one thing. A husband almost killing another man for touching his wife's feet is something else." So the constant linking of these words keeps the dialogue continuously flowing. Vincent then asks another question: "But did it happen?", to which she answers, "The only thing Antwan ever touched of mine was my hand, when he shook it at my wedding." Then she goes on to say that only Marsellus and Tony Rocky Horror know the truth of what happened. So the segment that began with the name Antwan ends with the name Antwan and she takes a sip of her shake. At that point, the segment effectively ends as the Ed Sullivan impersonator begins to talk about a dance contest.

Let's first address the number of links used in this segment alone:

promise	3x
offended	2x
forget	2x
Is that a fact?	2x
Antwan	4x
Tony/Rocky Horror	6x
Marsellus	4x
they	4x
and	2x
foot/feet/massage	4x
touched/touching	2x

four-story window	2x
seemed	3x
reasonable	2x
protective	2x
	44 Links

There are approximately twelve questions and sixteen statements that include statement leads and redirected statement leads. If we total the number of links in the entire scene (excluding Mia's brief visit to the rest room) there are a total of eighty-five links! Coincidental, no; contrived, yes, but contrived in a very skillful manner.

What one must ask at this point is the following: What has Tarantino presented to us in relation to dialogue writing and how has that altered in almost thirty years since *The Graduate*? Even though the film's length clearly goes against the Hollywood norm, the techniques Tarantino uses are practically the same that Buck Henry used almost three decades earlier. No matter how innovative one might suggest *Pulp Fiction* is, Tarantino uses certain techniques that tend to transcend time in relation to the quality of dialogue writing.

But you may ask: Is there a kind of formula for using these techniques? Should I use a certain number of statement leads and Q&As and, especially, dialogue links? Well, no, I don't suggest that you count them, thinking you need ten of one and a dozen of another and a certain number of links per scene, but one has to keep in mind that screen dialogue is not stage dialogue. Stage dialogue is generally independent of action. From Chekhov to Ibsen to Beckett to Mamet, stage characters are not necessarily precluded from talking a lot, but the parameters for stage dialogue are different than for screen dialogue and for that reason the techniques used by writers as diverse as Tarantino and Henry become vital. What you need to keep in mind is that these techniques work regardless of the writer using them. They work to keep the conversation flowing and to keep the character arc growing. The purpose of the dialogue is to be fluid even when the dialogue redirects the focus in another direction. What's lethal in writing dialogue is not that the talking stops, but that the talking rambles with no clear direction.

WORKS CITED

Henry, Buck. 1967. *The Graduate*. Los Angeles: Embassy/Lawrence Turman, PolyGram Video.

Stallone, Sylvester. 1976. *Rocky*. Los Angeles: United Artists Corporation.

Tarantino, Quentin. 1994. *Pulp Fiction*. New York: Miramax Books, Hyperion.

EXERCISE 1

Using the following scheme, pick three scenes from a favorite film and analyze the dialogue components, then take a scene from your own script and do the same.

	QA	QSI	QSL	QQL	SSL	L
SC 1						
SC 2						
SC 3						
SC 4						

What similarities do you find? What differences? What's lacking?

EXERCISE 2

Play a video you enjoy without the sound and attempt to write the dialogue for each character. Scrutinize the scene, anticipating what's happening based on how the plot has developed to that point. After the exercise, listen to the dialogue to see what was actually said versus what you've written. How is the dialogue the same? How does it differ? What are the techniques being employed by the screenwriter, and have you employed the same?

CONCLUSION
AND THE WINNER IS . . . ?

SO WHERE DO YOU GO FROM HERE? IN OTHER WORDS, AFTER ALL IS said and done, what kind of a screenplay should one write? Obviously a commercial one. But what is a commercial screenplay? Someone must know what a commercial screenplay looks like when one sees it or how else can one say it does or doesn't exist?

In my attempts at discovering that illusive commercial film, I decided to do some research. I took the top one hundred American film all-time box office leaders, then took the top twenty-five of those (adjusted for inflation). Then I decided to classify those films to see if they fell into one particular category or if there were crossover categories. I decided to use the categories of adventure (including mystery/thriller), quest, epic, human interest (which would include romance), and fantasy (animation) to see what I'd come up with. This is what I found:

1	*Gone with the* Wind	epic/HI/quest
2	*Star Wars*	adventure/quest
3	ET	quest/HI
4	*The Ten Commandments*	epic/HI/quest
5	*The Sound of Music*	HI/quest
6	*Jaws*	adventure/quest
7	*Dr. Zhivago*	HI/quest
8	*The Jungle Book*	fantasy/HI/quest

9	*Snow White*	fantasy/HI/quest
10	*Ben Hur*	epic/quest
11	*101 Dalmatians*	fantasy/HI
12	*Empire Strikes Back*	adventure/quest
13	*Return of the Jedi*	adventure/quest
14	*Exorcist*	fantasy
15	*The Sting*	HI/quest
16	*Raiders of the Lost Ark*	adventure/quest
17	*Jurassic Park*	adventure/quest
18	*The Graduate*	HI/quest
19	*Fantasia*	fantasy
20	*Godfather*	adventure/HI
21	*Forrest Gump*	HI/quest
22	*Mary Poppins*	HI/fantasy
23	*Lion King*	fantasy/quest/HI
24	*Close Encounters*	adventure/quest
25	*Sleeping Beauty*	fantasy/HI/quest

It's curious to note the number of films in which the notion of quest as we've talked about it plays a significant part. The results shouldn't be too startling, though, because most traditionally written stories demand a story line that initiates a problem to be solved or a question to be answered. And here is a rather fascinating relationship. You'll notice that the word *quest* and the word *question* obviously have the same root and the root means "to ask" or "to inquire." A quest, like a question, is something that needs to be answered. The latter may be answered in a word or a phrase; the former must be answered through experience. In almost all of these films, there is a question to be answered and, by virtue of the question to be answered, a quest to be taken. The protagonist in almost all of these films experiences some kind of transformation. Clark Gable in *Gone with the Wind*; Dustin Hoffman in *The Graduate*;

Robert Redford in *The Sting*; Harrison Ford in *Raiders*; Al Pacino in *The Godfather*; even Simba in *The Lion King*. And why is that? Because in order for a story to be resolved, there must be a clear ending, and a clear ending (as do quests) presupposes closure. Without closure there is a kind of fragmentation, and fragmentation does not do well on screen or at the box office. So if there is one thing I recommend that you always keep as the standard of your story, it would be that you ask yourself these three questions:

What is the question to be answered?

What is the quest the protagonist is on?

What is the arc the character has made?

In terms of structure, those three questions will keep you on track in organizing your ideas and structuring your script.

I want to close with an excerpt that you might find very interesting, and I want you to keep in mind the kind of film you may like to see and the kind of film you may like to write as you read it.

> [We have to] be aware that the appeal of the typical photoplay is still to the average person, to Mr. John Q. Public, and that no photoplay which fails to please him is likely to be very profitable or successful. The producer must reduce his art to the level of the least common denominator, he must "take the suffrage of the plot," he must interest Tom, Dick, and Harry—to say nothing of Mary and Kate . . . The American photoplay is and probably will continue to be a popular art, it must continue to make its appeal to the aforesaid Tom, Dick and Harry, and their sweethearts, wives and children. And to make this popular art a high and worthy art, capable of giving emotional kicks and thrills to the average while communicating delight and thoughtful admiration to those who have, in this respect at least, finer taste and sharper critical acumen, this, I submit, is the most serious problem of the American photoplay.

This excerpt is from a book titled *How to Write Photoplays* by John Emerson and Anita Loos, written not in this year or last year or even in this decade or the last, but in 1920—eighty years ago, only about two decades after film was invented, and seven years before sound. So even though we have all sorts of technical gimmicks, special effects, Dolby sound, digital resolution, and glossier color, we still have one thing that's remained the same: the story. And if the story doesn't fit into a more or less preconceived notion of how a story must be told, the story will probably fail as a screenplay.

In closing, I must be brutally honest about the craft of screenwriting . . . at least in the United States. You will probably read and hear a lot of things about screenwriting and how one should write what one feels and how important art is. That's all well and good, but, in fact, the movers and shakers in Hollywood aren't really interested in that and the irony is that the members of the Academy who want to nominate a picture that seemingly reflects something humanistic, since those awards are a reflection of the Academy and the people who compose the Academy, are not necessarily the same people who get the film produced. In general, producers could care less about the integrity of the film as long as it makes a profit. So what often happens to screenwriters is that they must temper what they write. You see, screenwriting is not like fiction writing. As a writer of fiction, one is the sole purveyor of one's words. If one can't find an outlet for them, one could, for a fairly minimal amount of money, publish them oneself. Not so with film—at least feature film. You can, of course, do what I did with some people, and make a film for absolutely nothing, for the sheer enjoyment of making it. And you can attempt to repeat the success of the *Blair Witch Project*, but in general filmmaking is also money-making and, to a great extent, is contingent on commercial appeal and not necessarily quality.

I once wrote a screenplay about the effects a mother's death had on her two young children and her husband. It was a film about adolescent grieving and single parenthood and coming of age and a lot of other things. The Sundance Institute, the Academy of Motion Picture Arts & Sciences, and the Writer's Guild East have recognized it, but, to this day, no one has ever produced it. Why not? Too much of this, too little of that; too much of one, too little of another. That's not unusual. It took Tesich eight years to get *Breaking Away* done, and arguably the finest script he ever wrote, an adaptation of Cormac McCarthy's *Blood Meridian*, still lies dormant on some agent's bookshelf. Richard Attenborough allegedly took twenty years to get *Gandhi* to the screen. So nothing is beyond possibility in

Hollywood and elsewhere, it's just that possibility is often located somewhere in the backlot of beyond.

It's the wise screenwriter who studies not only screenwriting, but
directing, lighting, sound, and so on in order to understand the synergis-
tic approaches to filmmaking; but it is the wisest screenwriter who understands that after all is said and done, she or he is still merely a minor
player within a colossal monopolized wheel of an industry that pays
homage to power and the dollar bill. But one should clearly remember
that even though people may scramble and sully your screenplay, the one
thing they can never take from you in contract or deed is your integrity,
and with that in your possession, all your scripts will be successful ones.

WORK CITED

Emerson, John, and Anita Loos. 1920. *How to Write Photoplays*. New York:
James A. McCann.